I HATE WHITE AMERICA

ASHLEY TOSE

iUniverse, Inc.
Bloomington

I Hate White America

iUniverse books may be ordered through booksellers or by contacting:

iUniverse
1663 Liberty Drive
Bloomington, IN 47403
www.iuniverse.com
1-800-Authors (1-800-288-4677)

ISBN: 978-1-4759-3162-4 (sc)
ISBN: 978-1-4759-3163-1 (ebk)

Library of Congress Control Number: 2012910261

Printed in the United States of America

iUniverse rev. date: 06/18/2012

Contents

Book I
I Hate White America

We Did It To Ourselves

⚠ *Warning* ⚠

This book was written based on the fact, opinion, and my point of view. If I offend you or you feel that I am politically incorrect PLEASE feel free to correct me in the privacy of YOUR OWN HOME.

Key: Those people = White people

Greatness is not given, but it's earned.

Barack Obama
Inauguration speech 2008

Did You Know?

- Thomas Jefferson wrote in the Declaration of Independence that slavery was a cruel war against human nature itself. Violating its most sacred rights of life and liberty but it never made it to the final copy.
- If the union had lost the Civil War slavery would not be abolished. With that as a truth: How much unfair treatment would have yoked African-Americans if they had lost the war.
- The first statue of liberty was a Black Women breaking out of bondage.
- That nearly every hate group in America targets Blacks. There are 1,018 active hate groups in America.
- States have spent more money on prisons than on higher education. That leaves the reality: Poor education = potential crimes. Why? America is ran on a economical system that requires money regardless of education and states neglect children at early stages then invest and spend money on prisons. Somehow they know that under educated teens and young adults will find themselves in prison.

- In 1989 studies showed that Blacks were arrested for illegal at 5x the rate of whites, even though whites used illegal drugs about the same. Blacks are charged under the 3 strikes law at 17x the rate of whites in L.A. and 13x in San Francisco.

Latinos got prison terms for drug offenses at 2x the rate for whites, while Blacks are 33% more likely to end up in the penitentiary on the same charge.

Reports have also revealed that federal drug charges, which send defendants to prison for 5 or more years, potentially on the same charge. 4 out of 10 Blacks get caught in the justice system.

- Democrats were fighting to prevent the passing of Brown vs. the Board of Education.
- Democrats were opposed to the March on Washington by Martin Luther King Jr.
- President Kennedy's brother wire-tapped and investigated Dr. King for suspicious of Communist ties.
- Dr. MLK Jr. was also considered "The most dangerous man in America by J. Hoover because of his ability to organize.
- Democratic Public Safety Commissioner Eugene "Bull" Conner took full responsibility for the ordering of the housing and police dog attacks on the civil rights protesters and the collective arrests for those extending constitutional rights of assembling without violence.
- Democratic governors were guilty of pro-segregation threats sent protesters and withholding integration from schools.

- 50% of all abortions are performed on Blacks; however the bodies are sold and profited off of.
- There are 1.37 millions abortions in America a year and 3,700 per day. 60% are white, Black women are 3x likely than white, and Hispanics roughly 2x as likely. 43% women have abortions by the age of 45
- The mafia, CIA, FBI, and military all took part in the assignation of Dr. MLK.
- George Crum—a Black man—invented the potato chip.
- In America there are:

  One murder every 22 minutes
  A rape every 5 minutes
  A robbery every 49 seconds
  A burglary every 10 seconds

AMERICA

I'm quite certain may are curious about the writer of this book. My name is Ashley—as it reads on the cover. I was born and raised in the state of Mississippi. My home state may help in explaining the title of this book because things in my state are still Black and white. I am fully aware that all whites are NOT the same and in writing this book I have put the entire race in the same category. Well that happens sometimes in America.

My reason for *"I Hate White America"* is things here in America have not changed much according to my calculation. Over time our nation has overcome many hurtles; however biased, opinionated, narrow minded thinking continue to delay progressions and hinder the American society. I constantly see all races—not just Blacks—being mistreated, misused, misunderstood and the list goes on—by the white race while movies, television shows, daily news reports, magazines, reality series, and the current news provide regularized visuals of racist America. Seems whites have not yet accepted that America is bigger than them. Problems and complications have yet ceased due to the measures and tactics that are made to ensure white racial supremacy. I decided to shed light on how that attitude affects my community. Issues between Black and white can dated back before slavery even existed and although hundreds of years have passed unsurprisingly some of these same issues are still issues of today.

I desire deeply that all may enjoy this book and that it would be an eye opener to all who read it or merely hear about it. We must all remember this book was written from my point of view and I intend to make no one feel guilty but if certain feelings begin to arise inside of anyone—Black or white—just know I wrote the way I felt.

Acknowledgements can be credited to my racist state, this delusional society, the world wide web, televisions, movies, magazines, and the book "White over Black.

DEEPLY ROOTED

CHAPTER 1

Whites' repulsions against Blacks can be dated back to around the late 15th century; when the issue of color did not contain as much complexity as it is today. In those times the issue of color was a quite simple one: The European connotation of beauty and—before the 16th century—the denotation of Black. Beauty in the Europeans eyes was Queen Elizabeth while the definition of Black during that time was displeasing.

Def: Queen Elizabeth—Pale white; white rose cheeks.

> Black—Deeply stained with dirt, soiled, dirty, foul . . . Having dark or deadly purposes, malignant, pertaining to or involving death; deadly, baleful, disastrous, sinister . . . Foul iniquitous, atrocious, horrible, wicked . . . Indicating disgrace, censure, liability, to punishment; of baseness and evil, and sign of danger and repulsion.

Clearly the appearance and beauty of Queen Elizabeth was incomparable to the Africans. The Africans facial features were significantly different from the Europeans and Africans were considered to be unattractive because of color, the fullness of lips, the broadness of the nose, and coarseness of hair. The preference of white over Black began with personal opinion. The bias outlook toward Africans was not held by all Europeans and began to raise questions. Some questioned: 1. Why were the people of a much darker complexion so distasteful when the color of one's skin remains under the control of no man. 2. Does the quality and value of a man differ by color? 3. Is white really better than Black?

Of course many Europeans at that point in history answered yes to the last two questions because they judged according to and in favor of what they looked like. The establishment and time length of slavery imbedded those bias thoughts and created a social boundary causing hatred among the two races.

LAND OF THE FREE

CHAPTER 2

Come one come all to the land of the free. Yeah . . . right. In the land of the free freedom is not free. Freedom comes with a high price and all those willing to pay, pay with their lives.

The founders of America knew how it felt to be under the control of others. America knew that every man yearned for freedom and liberty; if otherwise she would have never fought Great Britain for her independence. My question: Why is white America so reluctant in granting other races freedom, equality, liberty, and the pursuit of happiness to citizens of her soil? Since July 4, 1776 freedom and equality has been a never ending fight. Slaves fought the confederates, women fought the men, and the Blacks fought whites. Decades of inhuman, cruel, discriminative, and prejustice behavior has been inflicted on all except Caucasians. Documents in history were written favoring whites and/or banning Blacks. The DOI is a complete contradiction in itself.

"We hold these truths to be self-evident, that all men created equal, that they are endowed by their Creator with certain unalienable Rights that among these are Life, Liberty, and the pursuit of Happiness.

Well written; nonetheless, a bunch of BS. The second continental congress wrote the DOI in hopes to gain independence of Great Britain not caring that they themselves were tyrant to slaves. If white America truly believed that all men were created equal and are endowed inalienable rights—one of which is liberty—why were all men not independent on July 4, 1776???? Between then and now; documents and amendments have granted freedom to all men, but despite major advancements some 230 years later the Black community still does not feel "free." Rules regulations, laws, codes, mores, and folkways have been unfairly enforced upon Blacks since slavery.

The Black Code

The Black Code existed as the first statute of limitation that whites applied to the former slaves. Though they were free; most were illiterate and all were ignorant to the meaning of equality and the rights they were entitled to after the emancipation proclamation.

The Black Code stated:

1. if a Black was unemployed and without permanent residence they could be arrested and bound out for a term of labor if unable to pay fine. RED FLAG! The emancipation proclamation promised all slaves 40 acres and a mule. If the government had given them what they promised instead of selling dreams

it would be an unlawful arrest. Many had nowhere to go and no work. It's funny how former slaves could not find work but the whites had plenty of work if former slaves could not pay fines. This code made it extremely difficult for the Black community to be free and to survive.

2. Former slaves could not carry firearms. Slaves could not carry firearms because the whites feared massacres, serial killings, or violence. Blacks may have decided to take justice in their own hands, since any fair justice was unheard of in that period.

3. Former slaves could not testify in court if concerning whites, only if it concerned Blacks. A Black not being able to testify against whites gave whites a "Get out of Jail" free card. The period of the Black Code there were very few white on white crimes, opposed to white on Blacks crimes. Really look at it though: A white person could commit any act of criminal activity as long as Blacks were the witnesses and/or victim. Wow, "justice for all." White folks knew the dangers and extremes of holding people in bondage. Benjamin Franklin described slavery like holding a wolf by the ears: it's a bad position to be in but you better not let it go. He like many others had foreseen the negative effects of slavery that followed the Emancipation Proclamation.

Jim Crow

The Black Code was the introduction of the unfairness from white America towards Blacks in America. After the Black Code came Jim Crow. Jim Crow dominated society from 1877 until the Civil Rights Act of 1964. 87 years of "separate but equal." Nowhere in America was anything equal. Attitudes were negative, bias, and those people acted as if Blacks were unfit to become active members of society. There has and will always be a double standard in this country: men and women, blondes and brunettes, attractive people and unattractive people, rich and poor etc. Jim Crow laws just made separation, inequality, and mistreatment legal for whites. Ex: Blacks either could not enter the establishment or had to enter though the back door. Not only could whites come to Black establishments invited or uninvited, they could also deface and destroy properties. Sounds like separate and unequal and although "Jim Crow" is not in our present day laws; America still lives by it.

In the 1800s local and national government made laws to ensure white racial supremacy. Today local and national government still enforce the breaking and punishments of laws more heavily on Blacks than any other race. A lot of whites have the attitude that the land belonged to them. Lets be real. America could not be the America she is without the diverse contributions of every race and ethnic group that resides on her soil. She has never and still cannot be one of the greatest countries, function, and advance the way she does with only one race. People of all colors, shapes, and sized consider this land to be home. "We may have arrived on different ships, but we are all in the same boat"

CONTROL

CHAPTER 3

Due to conformity of both races and the profit whites were receiving from the free labor, slavery became the normal way of life for America; despite its unconstitutionality. Slavery had laid an uneasily shifted foundation but the Emancipation Proclamation forced America to undergo unexpected resocialization and changed society for better and for worse. Complaining and unwillingness stimulated from both parties, but without consideration this uninvited change had become inevitable.

The newly acquired freedom of slaves changed the norm of society compromising the rules and expectations that society was trying to ingrain in slaves. Appearance, manner, and conduct has so long been the decision of whites and the mere thought of "freedom for all" scared America. Slaves were illiterate human machines and for them to gain social independence was challenging the fundamental expectations that society had for Blacks. No racial competition existed leaving whites to feel superior. Slavery abolishment threatened whites muscle power over former slaves so they took whatever measures necessary to effectively exhibit where the former slaves fit in the new society. Written and unwritten rules, regulations, codes of behavior, and laws specified how procedures should be carried out, how individuals should behave, and what punishment or penalty should be imposed on those who disobeyed. Slave abolishment legally changed the social status of Blacks, but whites made sure Blacks social position remained the same and under whites' control. Those people also developed labels, social requirements, and institutions to protect their own interests. "Just because it had always been that way, did not and does not mean that it was the way it was supposed to be." Unsettled fear of equality for Blacks in America has left the community to deal with an unfair society that seems to want to keep them under social control no matter cost.

WRATH

CHAPTER 4

Many citizens of this country have a fear of the "Angry Black Man." He is a threat and dangerous to society. LOL. That notation always makes me laugh. Glancing back in history there has always been the "Angry white Man" who administers hatred and violence against any race of people other than himself. He held and entire race of people in bondage for 400 years using whips, shackles, illiteracy, and other cruel methods to maintain obedience and enslavement. The angry white man has created groups that center around hate and targets Blacks and all who are different. Rape, murder, beatings, bombings, and lynching provide crystal clear images of the actions taken by angry white men in the past for racial supremacy. How could the color of a man's skin and the want to be treated fairly make anyone so angry?? Have we not overcome those obstacles that have held our nation back for hundreds of years? Truthfully many whites are still angry and have the same racist attitude of their ancestors. Africans were bought to this country for specific reasons; work the land and bring profit. Whites never intended for slaves to become active members of society; let alone competition. Just think, had the free slaves really been granted 40 acres and a mule. A "Nigger" farmer making their own profit was a risk whites were not willing to take. Black men and women becoming independent somebody's when they were suppose all be a nobody made whites angry. In business, franchises, companies, and corporations—regardless of qualifications—Blacks position on the ladder only reach so high. Blacks obtaining power goes against the plan . . . bad enough those "Niggers" can vote. LOL. Racism and the people who practice it keep our country divided and hinder our society. Society does not like to accept or face the problems that those people construct out of hatred, jealousy, and anger. The angry white man provokes and is the reason for the angry Black men. Whites created the angry Black man from enslavement and years of unfair racist treatment. Whites also use Blacks and their noticeable anger as an excuse to punish Blacks.

CIVIL RIGHTS ACT OF 1964

The Civil Rights Act of 1964 contributed vitally to the advancement of this country and can be another book in itself. It showed the world how angry the white man really was and showed that America was never seeking for any real equality. Those people knew when they created "separate but equal" it was just another way to keep Blacks out their social and economic society. In what equal society is a race directed to step aside for another race but in return are stepped on and kicked? Some may view the CRA of 1964 as a rebellion but Blacks were doing what Jim Crow ordered. There were separate schools, neighborhoods, and social environments but if Blacks decided to enter white institutions they should have still receive equal treatment. Was there a need for apprehension, incarceration, brutal beatings, high pressured water hoses, and vicious attack dogs? Shame on the angry whites who organized these inhuman attacks. I thought that civil rights were more of those inalienable rights endowed by our Creator. Everyone has personal liberties allowing them to be free from the rule and control of others in our legal, economic, and social order; Blacks were asking to be given the rights entitled to them for being American citizens under the American Constitution. Had this non-violent movement never taken place those people would have continued with separate but equal.

KLU KLUX KLAN

One could not talk about hate in America and leave out the KKK. That would just be un-American. First let me applaud every single branch and organization that relates themselves to the KKK. Klan groups have grown to be one of the biggest hate organizations in America that target everyone except the average white person. I congratulate you because you all have gotten away with murder. Literally.

Since the establishment of the KKK there has been increases and decreases in members and activity but the existence has not yet ceased. White men still get a kick out of playing dress up in their wives sheets and dancing around a burning cross. As far as I know; gathering around a burning cross symbolizes their faith and the heated flames give them some kind of spiritual connection and energy. The KKK has given the word idiot a new definition entry. America has a bunch of bald white men prancing around in sheets spreading their hate for others . . . how great a country? It is common for an individual(s) to hate one person or a group of people, but to find friends to share the hate with and to purposely cause hurt and pain and/or death ranks at pure evil. People really hold meetings to discuss and plot against people whose only affliction is being different. In addition to the terror, Klansmen drag God name into the evil escapades making it even sicker. What Bible do they read from? This is not "Christian" faith. These are demon possessed people doing demonic work and rituals. The King James Version read versus that say "Let each of you look out not only for his own interests, but also the interests of others" and "love thou neighbor as thou self." There are no specifications and God has always stood for love NOT hate.

America seems to have little concern about this; Klans are still active in committing hate crimes. When murders, bombings, and lynching were taking place; no justice took place. In the 21st century investigations remain open and unsolved, trails are ongoing, souls have been lost and forgotten, and convictions are still being handed out for crimes committed decades ago. America's pledge last 5 words read "And justice for all." How unbelievable is that?

- **The United Klans of America** was the most prominent unit of the KKK in America.

- **The Christian Knights of the KKK**
  Formal 1985 active in North and South Carolina, Kentucky, and Tennessee. Once the suspect in 2 June 1995 arsons of predominantly Black South Carolina churches.
- **The Keystone Knights of the KKK**

Break away function form the Invisible Empire of the KKK. The Keystone Knights publish anti-Jewish and anti-Black newsletter called "The Keystone America."

- **The Knights of the KKK (Arkansas Fraction)**
  Founded 1975. Largest and most active Klan fraction operating in the nation today. There has been a decline in membership.

- **The Knights of the KKK (Michigan Fraction)**
  Low profile Klan group

- **Federation of Klan's; Knights of the KKK**
  Formed in 1994. Little to no organizing. Average 50 members across 50 states.

- **Knights of the White Camellia KKK**
  Based out of Texas. Formed in 1867. This Texas branch has been linked to a number of incidents of racial intimidation and harassment in Vidor, Texas. The Texas commission of Human Rights has brought a civil suit against Klan groups in response to these incidents. Aragon Nation HOW TO JOIN—Requirements for membership are simple. You must be 100% White, have an open mind to learn Christian Identity and be willing to follow Klan rules and regulations.

- **Aragon Nation**
  A hatred group of Christian identity. Northern Europeans whites and their American descendants are the "chosen." They believe Jews are the synagogues

13

of Satan; Blacks and other people of color are subhuman "mud people" land homosexuals should be executed. Organizations host semi-annuals at its headquarters. They have a prison outreach ministry that is affiliated with Aragon Brotherhood prison gangs. They have a website and is the most significant "identity" oriented organization in America.

- **Militias**
  Went public in 1994. Militia organizations now operate in at least 40 states. Their membership totaling as many as 15,000, out numbering skinheads, neo-Nazi and the KKK combined. They particularly hate Jews.

- **National Alliance**
  The neo-Nazi National Alliance is the most sophisticated best organized, and best financed overtly Hiliterian Organization in the U.S. Are responsible for the 1995 Oklahoma City bombing. Associated with some of America's most violent right-wing terrorists. They denounce Jews, Blacks, brown, and yellowing parasites. They use propaganda to attack gays lesbians, women, feminism, and even the disabled

- **Skinheads**
  Neo-Nazi skin head in the U.S. have been responsible for at least 41 murders since Dec. 1987. Racist skinheads partake in bigotry and are purely ethnically prejudice. They are accountable for several murders and countless assaults against

gays and lesbians. This organizations even has anti racist dreams of organizing a race war in the U.S.

- **White Aryan Resistance**
  Leading in information and propaganda clearing house for the neo-Nazi skinhead movement in the U.S. They create propaganda against Jews, Blacks, and other groups. Record of voice holds attention of enforcement and the condemnation of the public.

What conclusions can be drawn after reading all the different organizations and their intentions? RACISM AND HATE CONTINUE TO RAGE ON IN AMERICA. Americans seat and watch the news and believe the news anchors as they report the latest stories and never really questioning what they hear. People are out there creating flamboyant stories with the hopes of imbedding prejudice thoughts and discriminative acts against people they choose to hate. There are a countless number of crimes that have been committed against innocent people yet no real justice has been served. White America is angry and are the dangerous people. But because of propaganda and government assistance these organizations are free to rein fear, hatred, and commit crimes on any group they choose. The Internet blogs and comment sections of websites show America how angry and/or racist white America really is. It makes no sense how blind America tries to act when racism is the topic of conversation. Stop trying to sell that lie. As we all can see there are groups and groups of people who spend time out of their lives to ensure unpleasant problems and obstacles on innocent taxpaying AMERICAN CITIZENS.

EQUALITY vs. HISTORY

CHAPTER 5

Equality

Black people have gone to extremes to enter into the white community. Blacks aspire and conform to those people's way of life because they consistently lie and sell one dream after another to the Black community. Despite the deceit and compulsiveness of lies, my community keep allowing themselves to be sucked into believing damn near each and every lie.

America's 1st lie: Separate but equal. White folks where selling the dream that they and Blacks would live in America have separate everything but still be treated equally after a history of slavery. After that lie was unveiled then came the lie of a integration. Many may wonder; how was integration a lie?? It depends on the way one looks at it. Believers of the lie probably think/thought this: Integration changed America for the better. Blacks were welcome in the same environment as whites. It puts Blacks and whites on a more balanced scale of equality. Ok. Here is my truth of integration."

Integration made it easier for white people to mistreat Blacks. Blacks invaded whites territory and it put Blacks on whites terms. It also showed that whites never cared to know Blacks and their culture. Blacks integrated the white's schools, churches, neighborhoods, and establishments. If Blacks integrate into white America it is/ was considered a step up but considered a step down if whites integrate into Black America. Whites allowing Blacks to integrate was another way to profit. When it comes to money America becomes color blind; she only sees GREEN. KEEP THE RICH RICH AND THE POOR POOR. After Blacks spend their money with white businesses, they pocket the money and spend it to keep their people in the superior and best looking position. Enlightening because the Black community will go into the poor house trying to live like white America. Black people know those people better than they know themselves. How . . . because of history.

History

History plays an important role because it teaches us about the past and helps us to alter the future. History exposes the flaws, mistakes, and triumphs of those before us giving us an advantage to better sculpt the present and future. Without learning history; history will continue to repeat itself. Ignorance to the past leaves us confused as individuals, lost as communities and groups, and divided as a nation.

Black people must take responsibility because our community lives dumb to the history of our people and culture. Blacks live ignorant to the past partly because we do not take our time to learn it ourselves or take the time to teach it to our children; But that is not withstanding toward why the Black community and the world are unaware of the past. The true history and dirty laundry of America is left out of the history books. Yes, the entire 28/29 days of February center around the history of my people but the first of March begins a new month and the teaching of Black history ends. Black history month does not give enough time to learn or teach ones history and month will not hurt all those opposed to it. White history, on the other hand, receives the remaining school calendar months. People tend to wonder racism still exists and history books play a major role in the answer they may seek. For centuries history books only record one detail about Blacks in history. Slavery holds an entire in-depth discussion in history books across America then blacks fade away until the Civil Rights Movement. Authors try and capture the success of America's history and not the truth. Black history has to searched for and Black authors, artist, and poets reveal the truth about Black history. "American History" is the learning course taught through out elementary, middle, and high school; making it a mandatory course judged on a grading scale in order to receive the diploma that America urges all students to receive.

To an uninformed mind, white people founded and built this country single handedly. Black inventions and contributions fill very few chapters, sections, paragraphs, and sentences. "What you are is what you will always be," goes unsaid but is the reality of how white America view the Black community; acting as if Blacks will never be more than servants with poor literacy skills- since that is how the history book portray Blacks. African "Americans" were inventors, had progressions and downfalls, successes and disappointments through our history as well any other American community. At predominantly white schools Black history is not celebrated at all; or at least not the "white" school I graduated from. At Clinton High School there was not one program organized, no bulletins or posters plastered, or even announcements made. I, of course, asked the current principal why were things that way. His response was that Black history was incorporated into our everyday year round studies. I wanted to protest but I noticed that it was nothing new to the students and Black History month did not matter. America is robbing students of this month because American History is white history. One month or one day is unfair to minorities. History books are more tactics of deceit and another illusion in equality.

History and equality go hand in hand. Whites are teaching all who attend school in this country only what they want them to know; though every race, ethnic group, culture, and religion have played some type of roll in America's success. No matter who did what, whites make sure they receive recognition. On the other hand, when things go wrong in America whites waste no time in putting the blame on any/every one else. America is great; her history is just filled with corruption, lies, and deceit. The future picture of America is grim and dim if things continue on the path that has been lead.

ITS UGLY HEAD

CHAPTER 6

PART 1

Racism-the belief that race is a primary determinant of human traits and capacities and that racial difference produce an inherent superiority of a particular race.

America wants one to believe that racism has become a figment of the imagination. Racism is a past issue and the Black community has no justification to report such activity and these actuations can easily be explained with paranoia, delusion, and/or crying wolf. America reports that racism lived once but no longer exists in her melting pot society. That type of hatred is not alive in this day and time.

As asinine as that may sound people have been convinced into actually believing that. "Paranoid and delusional," you gotta be kidding me? The none racist whites believe it because many whites have never experienced first hand racism and give the accused the benefit of the doubt. Others cannot relate and instead of seeking an understanding;

people choose to block out the thought of racism still being a problem after all these decades. Racism goes unnoticed, unchallenged, unseen, and unexposed. Things being coincidental, exaggerated, or misinterpreted, are more cushioning possibilities than racism. Racist individuals and groups rely on the myth that racism no longer exists. When racist activity takes place and questions begin to rise; those people flip the script and make people doubt themselves. Case and point: Black people are paranoid.

To white non-racist who may have been mistaken as racist I ask that you would please forgive my people. One must understand our past and our present. My community often falls victim to racism (or know someone who has) leaving us with clouded judgment. Blacks are not paranoid; just skeptical. Living in this country and being targeted by racist; POC are on guard (sub) consciously because whites can be sneaky, knifing, and deceitful. White people put on their "I love everyone" faces before they brush their teeth; explaining the skepticism.

I may be one of my people with clouded judgment. Being from the Mississippi, things here remain Black and white and the state is still not all that happy about segregation. There is a double standard based on race and Blacks are still not treated equally as whites. I worked, lived, and attended school in Clinton, Ms and got a first hand look of racism, prejudice, and discrimination. Many Blacks; especially males, do not like to enter the city of Clinton because of the harassment and treatment from the local police. I worked in local stores and dealt with racist customers on a regular basis. Some whites would rather be lost and confused instead of asking a Black employee for help. Customers purposely ignore the cashiers out reach for the money; to place it on the counter here is a sign of disrespect. Some customers will throw the money at the cashier and some refuse to speak back after being greeted by employees. The city of Clinton, Hinds county, Rankin county, and Madison county, and the State of Mississippi are not the only places racism dwells. This entire country; in some shape, form, or fashion have angry racist reining racism on every corner at every given chance.

Part 2

Prejudice—preconceived judgment or opinion. 2. Adverse opinion or option formed beforehand without grounds or before sufficient knowledge. 3. Irrational attitude of hostility directed against an individuals, a group; or supposed characteristics.

Prejudice can be tricky because it can simply be ones preference of one thing over another. Prejudice is also more common and exercised than the average person thinks. We are all prejudice in one way other another. Let me explain: Here in Ms my whole life I would always here Black people say "Prejudice white folks," therefore I always believed white folks were prejudice and racist. Though it was true on many levels; when I looked at the word and the definition more in depth I found the entire country has prejudice tendencies. A global look at prejudice is nationalism

Nationalism—a sense of national consciousness exalting. One nation above all others and placing primary emphasis or promotion of its culture and interest as opposed to those of other nation.

Wars around the globe start on the account that one religion, tribe, country, even ones thoughts are better than others. Our country's citizens are prejudice based on culture, personal and religion beliefs, and physical features. In our society people are prejudice for no fundamental reason. American citizens are prejudice toward illegal aliens because according to our country's guidelines they do not belong. Since the land was forcefully overtaken by white European sailors, who really has he say of who belongs and who does not? Religions keep up an ongoing debate. No religion is better even if the religion do not believe in the same God. People materially rich are prejudice and discriminate against the materially poor. A more unconscious level of prejudice is propaganda. Propaganda ranks number one in causes of prejudice attitudes, discrimination, and racism. Most things viewed on television and the Internet is a bunch of B.S. Due to falsefulness of propaganda, sufferance is the affect on the nation. A prejudice outlook is simple minded, ignorant, and petty but the way of life for America.

There is only one type of currency in America. A $10 bill is the same bill no matter who holds it. It can buy anything anywhere in America as long as it fits in the $10 price range. The value of the bill will not appreciate or depreciate upon the holder. So why in some situations do people act as if it does? In Mississippi Blacks are always receiving "You are not suppose to be here" or "Why are you people here" looks from whites whenever we choose to go to their preferred restaurants or places of business? A person's money is as good as the next but in America's society it's a blur; despite the same dead president face rest on the bill, those people still find away to exercise prejudice attitudes. It does not end at money. Streets are made basically from the same materials. What is the difference from a Black person riding on it than a white person? Remember our forefathers stated that all men were created equal. Why can we not be treated as such? Guess it is too much like right. The moment a person excludes another person based on their biased way of thinking is discrimination. I was taught that all men were created equal and in God's image. So people who look different may just be another image of God. ***Most of the things people hold against one another can either be taken away or cannot be changed.***

Watch your thoughts because they become your words
Watch your words because they become your actions
Watch your actions because they become your destiny

This wisdom has played itself into a negative dreadful destiny in America generation after generation. Love, hate, prejudice, and discrimination begin with thoughts. Society has created a dark doomed destiny for us, our children, and the world.

Part 3

Discrimination—treatment or consideration of or making a distinction in favor of or against, a person or thing based on the group, class, or category to which that person or thing belongs rather than on individual merit.

Prejudice thoughts equal discrimination. People deal with discrimination and mistreatment in this country and do not deserve it. There is racial, religion, and cultural discrimination on the news, in magazines, on television, in the work place, in schools, and on the streets routinely based on prejudice thoughts and racist feelings. Discrimination= racism and/or superior thinking. Discrimination due to hatred come from selfish thinking. Gossip and hear say drive a lot more discrimination and people in this country (especially the Black community) are emotionally beat down and judged off preconceived notations. People are demoted, fired, harassed, talked about, and laughed at. Prejudice thoughts make discrimination as simple as not associating or to stop associating with people based on personal opinion. America labels different races, stick them with stereotypes, then criticize its culture, make fun to their language/ slang, and judge its culture/way of life according to what she thinks and the way she thinks it should be. News and biased experiences are shared around the country through hearsay. General approaches can be taken toward groups' and races of people but in American society those thoughts and feelings lead to disassociation (discrimination) and friends who feel the exact same way. Discrimination plays in the work place, schools, social interactions, and words, racial slurs, phrases, and name calling are afflicted on people of all ages, shapes, and sizes. Discrimination causes harm, hurt, and injury to American citizens. Discrimination leads to a bigger picture and influencing the thoughts of society pull the strings of racial superiority. Racism, prejudice, and discrimination help in evil tactics toward minorities. This corrupts and divides society.

THESE COLORS DON'T . . .

CHAPTER 7

The American military act as a security and rescue system for many nations and protect and serve upon call. America can act as a protector for other countries but not for herself. America's military soldiers are treated like mindless robots who must obey every command of the government no matter the underline reason behind the command. In a nation full of lying, deceiving, money hungry politicians; who knows the logistics of our nation's orders. America does not even for fill the promises she makes to soldiers upon their return home from war. A soldier's decision to enlist affects the entire family. America's leaders have no regard for this; concerns are mostly greedy desires rather the than the long term causes and effects of all those dead soldiers. The war on terrorism left our country suffering and it appears that people in government and large companies reaped healthy sums though insurance, borrowing and lending, and invading the land of others. The people who declare these wars and sign off on bills NEVER step foot on the battlefield and if so are surrounded by body guards. Political leaders wives do not worry about losing a husband and their children do not worry about losing a father; so they do not understand the price of fighting for good 'ol America. The war in Iraq not really war; its American soldiers on foreign land enforcing America's way of government on them. The way the middle Easters run their society is bizarre, drastic, and violent; however has nothing to do with the real problems in America.

**Africa is Bizarre, drastic, and violent ordeals transpiring and civil wars are carrying one and America is not rushing to rescue the innocent. Women are being raped, beaten, and killed; children are being held captive, forced to join civil wars, addicted to drugs and violence, and diseases are taking numberless lives. America is not lending her helping hands. Sexually assaulted African women travel long ways and wait weeks in hopes to receive womb care because of brutal attacks but there are no commercials asking for help to build hospitals. Wonder why? Lets see . . . how can America benefit from a bunch of Africans infected with Aids and killing each other with machine guns and chopping people up with machetes. She can't. After Africans destroy each other; America and Europe will work together to over throw what is left of the continent is my speculation.

The amounts of deaths and the poverty level mean nothing to America. Society traditionally defines a person by possessions and/or power one holds, leaving the rich vs. the poor in a divided society. A large percentage of America is poor and the wealthy and well connected run the inherited wealth keep the same people, customs and beliefs systems in charge. America reveals itself as a deceiving democratic liberty with injustice and victimizes citizens into a subconscious monarchy. The soldiers are merely henchmen that enforce written and unwritten rules, regulations, codes of behavior, laws, procedures, and punishment or penalty on those who disobey America's government. These colors don't care about the soldiers or the citizens.

Military suicide rates:

-American soldiers are taking their own lives in the largest number since records began to be kept in 1980. 128 confirmed in Army: 41 in Marines; 15 under investigation. There is an average of 10 failed suicide attempts for actual loss of life. Some sources figures suggest than 1600 army and marine personal tried to kill themselves in 2009. Estimated 30% of soldiers who took their lives in 2008 did while on deployment and another 35% committed suicide after returning from duty. Dozens of men and women have left the armed forces since serving in Afghanistan or Iraq also committed suicide in 2008. Department of Veterans Affairs has recorded 144 such cases. Suicide among 20 to 24 was 22.9 per 100,000in 2007. 4x that than non-veterans in the same age range. A hotline for veterans has received over 85,000 calls since mid 2007 and arranged some 2,100 suicide prevention interventions. Civilians are taking their own lives over the economic crisis. 11.1 deaths per 100,000 are equal to 33,300 suicides per year. People all over the nation are suffering from depression, emotional illnesses, mental illnesses, and decide end all the agony and pain they face in America.

RACISM IN THE MILITARY:

The military, like the rest of America, is racist and discriminates. Many Black soldiers are not receiving the recognition and rank they deserve. Those people keep up the battle of envy, jealousy, and/or hate within themselves because of having to follow the commands of a Black with rank, power, and leadership. America and her henchman air commercials and make empty promises to my community by persuading them to sign their life away and fight for a country that left the city of New Orleans under water; for a country that continues to mistreat Black America, for a military that does not judge and promote fairly. My community tells one another "The army aint no place for a Black man," history and that saying have proved itself true.

World War I

No Blacks were allowed in the Marines, Coast Guard, Air Force, and allowed in Navy only as mess men (dining room work). Before the draft there were 4 Black regiments and they were not used over seas in combat. When the draft began; more than Blacks registered: 31% were accepted in comparison of 26% whites. Black women offered their help and services as nurses and were denied. Blacks were told to tear off a corner of their registration cards so they could easily be identified and inducted separately (like America would have had it any other way). Southern postal workers deliberately withheld the registration cards of eligible Black men and would then have them arrested for being draft dodgers (racism and hatred). By the end of WWI the duties of Blacks evolved very little because Black men were still unable to serve in combat units and although they would earn higher positions; the Army was not handing out equal treat between those men and Black men. White soldiers would refuse to salute Black officers and rarely was there when whites were insubordinate. Discrimination was over looked or condoned and Black were banned from the officers clubs and quarters. The rules read that no more than 1/4 of Army trainees could be Black with the War Department's signature stamped at the bottom. Blacks went without proper clothing and were assigned complimentary old civil war uniforms. In those out dated uniforms; Black soldiers were forced to sleep outside in pitched tents; some were forced to eat outside during the winter months; others went with a change of clothes for months at a time; some force/ tricked into working 24 hrs straight based on special privilege promises. *Not all soldiers during this time dealt with those conditions* And with all the problems Black soldiers faced; whites feared that Black soldiers would return demanding equality as Black men and thought they might try and do so with their military training. Those racial assumptions resulted in racial terrorism during the summer of 1919. Anti-Black race riots erupted in 26 cities across America and the lynching of Blacks increased form 58 in 1918 to 67 in 1919. That summer at least ten were war veterans and some were lynched in their uniforms.

In the mix of the world wars and the terrifying holocaust, Black in Germany dealt with the war on racism as well. Interracial relationships and child reproduction posed itself as a threat to the purity of the German race. Views of such nature resulted in discrimination and isolation socially, and economically. During the holocaust Blacks were abducted as prisoners of war, placed in concentration camps, incarcerated, isolated, brutally murdered and persecuted, sterilized, and used as lab rats for medical experimentation.

World War II

Nearly one million Blacks were faced with racial discrimination and the military maintained a racially segregated military. Blacks were often classified as unfit for combat and were not allowed on the front lines. They were given mostly support duties and not allowed in the units with the white soldiers until 1914. The Blacks civil rights leaders convinced the government to setup all Black units as an experiment to see if Blacks could perform military task at the same level of white soldiers; of course the experiment proved to America and her military that Black soldiers were more than capable to perform military task at eh level of whites.

-Woodrow Crockett was apart of the Tuskegee Airman-the first group of Black pilots ever trained by the Air Force. They flew 149 missions during 1944-1945 and never lost a man in fire.

-The Double V was a double victory for Black soldiers. 1. Victory was against enemy abroad and the 2nd was a victory at home—America—against racism, discrimination, prejudice, and Jim Crow.

-African American scientist and technicians contributed to the success of defense weaponry created for WWII. Blacks made major contributions but interviews, document, new reports, and pictures left out the African American men and women who help achieve the goals and accomplishments and once again white America walked away in history as if it was done single handedly. America disregarded the titles, status, and earned pay of Black scientist, technicians, and mechanics by handing out guides showing where they were allowed to stay and eat. After the war these same highly skilled, trained, and experienced scientist, mechanics, and technicians were still unable to find jobs.

-President Truman ordered integration in 1948 and some how Black soldiers remained in separate units during the Korean War. It was not until the Vietnam War of the 1960s and 1970s the military fully integrated. Ironically; Black soldiers were considered to be fighting two wars during Vietnam.

Blacks efforts through out history and all the drama that came with it; Black soldiers have help write American history and have helped in America's success and it goes unrecognized and unappreciated. Regardless of rank Blacks endured so much of America's mistreatment; yet Black men and women continued to join the fight for America and her success. That bitch has a marvelous way of showing her appreciation. These colors don't care what Blacks have done for this country. If America remains in a racist state of mind then so does the military. As long as the military is racist "the army ain't no place for a Black man."

UNITED WE STAND, DIVIDED WE FALL

The average white person is dense. They are so often distracted and focused on themselves and their bias beliefs that they have lost sight of the bigger picture. America's division could very well be here down fall. America's history has periods of wars but none bleed on American soil and there was indirect conflict despite direct initiation. Had a country declared war on America, she would have not noticed because Americans are to busy declaring war on one another. Why did Blacks get mistreated and discredited in the army, ignore the history of injustice toward Black

America, still join the army, and never become terrorist? African American (Black men especially) fought for this country when she fought against them. Black soldiers live on and uphold their promise they made by suiting up and standing up for a racist country. Personally; i would not fight let alone die for a country that threats my entire race as if we are beneath them and the opposed only defense is our skin is Black. I may have gone out on missions and "accidentally" shot white racist soldiers. Bizarre? Not as bizarre as white veterans viciously murdering Black soldiers on their arrival home from war. Luckily Black soldiers don't think like me and white racist murderers and they dealt with the inequality and mistreatment so that America could continue to be the land of opportunity. In the end we are all one race . . . human. And one kind of people . . . American

☺ *HAPPINESS* ☹

CHAPTER 8

The pursuit of happiness is easier said than done for my community. A fight for happiness sounds more appropriate. Happiness would be a little easier to obtain if there was not a double standard. ABC 20/20 did a field experiment called "What would you do/ Racism in America" and it free to view on YouTube.com (part1&2). The experiment tested the reactions of white joggers witnessing the destruction of someone's property between a group of Black teens and a group of white teens doing the exact same thing and compared the responses and the number of 911 calls. The reactions were controversially different; revealing racism in America.

Black women are often mistakenly categorized as loose, fast, hoes, ghetto, and bitches mostly because rap music and music videos portray women smiling, laughing, dancing, and partying while artist rap with name-calling and degrading speech. This over-opioniated misconception explain part of why America looks down on the Black community. Record sells hold the truth to the misrepresentation and the abusive language but America does not think; she only judges. Riddle me this: if ALL Black women are hoes because some Black men say so and that is what America believes what are white women on the Girl Gone Wild commercials and DVDs? The commercials advertise a bunch of drunken white girls flashing their breast, exposing their vagina, and displaying lesbian behavior and its even for sale and America's cable networks have no problem airing the sales pitch.

Jena 6 were a group of Black teenage boys who were suspended and jailed because of a gang fight at school with white children. The fight transpired because the whites hung a nonce from a tree on school property. No school officials punished the students for the nonce hanging not did anyone take it down.—Imagine the treatment of the Black students from not only white students but also white faculty and staff.—Unsurprisingly a fight eventually erupted and the punishment for the Black students was jail. One Black teen was jailed for 9 months before the story hit headlines and major news. 9 months of jail for a fight at school weighs a heavy punishment for anyone. The justice system and those people who designed it have a 256 day rule enabling them to keep any arrested persons in jail for up to 256 before their day in court. And the municipal court system wanted to try and trail him as an adult. Outrageous! It is the 21st century and Blacks are still marching and fighting for fairness in the courts(the fight never really ended). MSNBC air footage of whites harassing, beating, and torturing one another and most arrested got off scotch free or with a slap on the wrist because the courts thought about the future and education of the guilty. Damn, I wish our Black men could get that thoughtful consideration from the justice system.

Dave Chappell did a comedy segment and he asked the question "how old is 15?" He gave several examples of some double standards between Blacks and whites. One does not have to look very hard or very far for evidence of double standards and who is most likely to come out with the short end of the stick. Double standard discrimination happen everyday and everywhere and non whites suffer the most. How can we pursue happiness? Society mistreats and devalues our children, misguide and misuse our men, and expect the Black community to continue to settle for straps.

African Americans literally have to fight to make any progress in this country. We have to work harder, study longer, sing louder, dance better, know more, run faster, and basically be exceptional at everything we achieve on the road to happiness. The American Dream is even a double standard and Americans are blind. She sees what she wants and ignores what she does not. Her vision changes according to favor not truth. Right, wrong, and fairness have no color, shape, size, or gender. Transgressions for a man or women, Black or white, Christian or Buddhist should all be measured the same yet are not. Society tells us that things differ according to circumstances and America does not bother herself with fairness because she will always be right.

THE MAN

CHAPTER 9

When Blacks use the phrase "The Man," most of the time they are not talking about one specific white man who keeps the entire race of Black people down; they are referring to the white race. White males run this land we call America. The most rich and powerful people are not famous. White men run the corporations that do not allow other races a fair chance at climbing the corporate ladder. The "white man" are supervisors and managers that act as if they own employees and take advantage of those they who are ignorant to company policies; white men who are high in white collar jobs, overpaid, know absolutely nothing, and are always seeking help from their employees; white men whose hands never get dirty, know nothing about hard work, and look down on the blue collar working class; white men who discriminate and categorize people solely on appearance, attire, religion, and maybe even hand writing. White women fall into the "white man" as well. There are the white women who turn up their nose to anyone who cannot afford to shop in the same bouquets; white women who cannot stand to be lightly brushed by anyone who is not in the same social class; white women who still think their race should remain majority; white women who give to the less fortunate out of pity instead of the heart; white women who walk around posing as humanitarians when the truth of the matter was because people were looking.

People can say: But we have a Black President. My remark to that: Barack Obama was elected America's 44th president; however he is one person and he deals with issues on a national and international level. He is not the first president nor will he be the last with more than one race in his bloodline. The 2008 election *will* change American history as we know it but it will not change the history that has already been written on the hearts and souls of every American. I felt like most Black people when he was elected nonetheless Obama is one man; he is not immortal nor is he a superhero here to save the world. The man who did that was Jesus. Many people have gotten it twisted; Obama is not super-save-a-hoe, he is a president like any other working to build a better America.

America's "white man" chases profit. Compassion and understanding about financial situations are not the worry of the MAN. He only aims to find different means to make himself richer. His tactics are efficient and some have even become traditional. Holidays are the biggest money makers that keep the MAN in business. Americans take out loans, over spend, and go into debt for holidays and celebrations.

I Christmas

As a child I anticipated Dec. 25 each year because since I was a baby I thought that a fat white man in a red suit would come to my house-only if I was a good girl—on a sleigh lead by reindeers to bring me presents. It was great until I realized 1. There is no such thing as Santa Clause and the cookies and milk we put out were eaten by my step dad. 2. All it does is put people in a financial bind. Children beg parents for presents that they cannot afford and over priced, employees pull names with price limits on gifts and people try to buy for family and friends while try to keep their head above water. 3. People pretend that they like you. Fake smiles and guilt gifts are given. Unfortunate families become charity cases, unfortunate children are made fun of because they lack all the new gadgets and clothes. And all of it is overrated. The illusion of Christmas is based on Biblical pretenses; the birth of Jesus Christ. The truthfulness of the exact date and month remains in question and the Bible teaches us to give from the heart all the time not just one month out of 12 or 1 day out of 365. Murder, fights, crimes, and deceit play along with the celebration of Jesus' "birthday." America will take Christ out of everything except the things that bring the dollars in. I don't know where Santa Claus and the North Pole originated from but it is a stupid concept. Americans are lying to children at early ages and misguiding on the road to life. Holidays like Christmas are the stepping-stones into the brain washing process of America. Santa rearranged is Satan. There is also a dark side to the Christmas holiday and people celebrate it in the name of Satan.

II 4th of July

"We hold these truths to be self-evident, that all men are created equal; they are endowed by their Creator with inherent and inalienable rights that among those are life, liberty, and the pursuit if happiness." DOI

Today the entire country recognized July 4th the day that America gained her independence. And yes, today anyone who lives here LEGALLY are given life, liberty, and the pursuit of happiness; however July 4·1776 when the 2nd conventional congress wrote the document they were not referring to *all* men, they were referring to only white ones. Recognizably, if America had never fought for independence, America—regardless of color—would not be free and the country would not be what she is today. July 4, 1776 "America" gained independence but the civil war did not began until April 12, 1861 ending May 10, 1865. That would leave Blacks in slavery for an additional 85 years after "independence" day. Blacks should have a separate day to celebrate independence.

America spends a lot of money to celebrate; becoming patriotic with flags and different attire and miscellaneous resemblances of red, white, and blue, food purchases for cook outs and fire works for entertainment for fun take place in the celebration of white men gaining independence. Never did those men expect slaves to be free or women to have equal rights as they did. Those white men wanted to be able to rule and control the way Great Britain ruled and controlled them without having to share profit or be held accountable for mistreatment and inequality. The historical holiday deserves acknowledgement yet is overrated.

III Easter

Every year Easter is celebrated on Sunday and everyone dresses up in their Sunday best and head the church even the people who have not attended church since the previous year on Easter Sunday. Oddly people feel obligated to attend church on this day because of the Biblical significance. If that is true where does the Easter bunny come from? Americans lie about another imaginary character and convince children to believe and spend money. Eggs, dye, Easter baskets, candy, food, clothes, and shoes are items purchased for the celebration of Jesus rising from the dead. Companies sell items that have no spiritual significance yet plaster the sacred names of God and Jesus and the symbol of crucifixion on superficial products. Easter has America twisting biblical holidays and pretenses to bring profit. The consumer market and believers help in the problems. People ignorantly cherish the useless items which brings idolism. In addition to idolizing; one Sunday of one month out of 12, believers make sure they look there best. God does not say come as you are except on Easter Sunday. Churches are filled to capacity with people who are there for more reasons than the celebration of Christ. The Christian faith has become watered down with ungodly traditions leaving non-believers with misinterpretations; leaving the truth muzzled; and leaving Satan to receive the glory. Easter baskets, egg hunts, and imaginary bunnies are a mockery to the Resurrection Day Celebration

What's the Difference?

IV Valentine

Valentines Day history is unclear but like most holidays it started out as something completely different than what it is today. The present day Febuary14 celebrations are filled with candy, cards, jewelry, restaurant outings, flowers, balloons, stuffed animals, expensive gifts, and evenings out making it finically beneficial to companies varying in product. Love is the supposed main element of this holiday but now has been transformed to focus on gifts and the price tag that follows. 21st century valentine day is outrageous! Society is blinded and Americans are not realizing that we are encouraging our children and adolescent relationships. Americans are also teaching that gifts are more about price tags that the thought and we are given unconscious consent to begin dating before they are truly ready. Valentines Day has also created a love façade. This display of fabricated love leaves lost conflicted impressions on easily impressionable people. Valentines Day unveils the lies told and the bad intentions we have for one another. People do not know the true meaning, feelings, or real display of love and V-day keeps them lost in confusion. Love in America has forever been misrepresented and what better plot of evil than to make a holiday celebrating fictional love.

V Halloween

America is aware that Halloween is related to fear, death, and demonic horrors yet year after year there is a celebration. Halloween has a long dark history and religious people incoherently ignore that this is obviously a pagan holiday. Halloween began originally as "All Hallows

Eve" and was celebrated by a group of people who made human sacrifices and worshipped idol gods. Among the gods was Saman; the god of death. The non-participants were afraid and believed that on Oct. 31st ghost, spirits, fairies, witches, and elves came out to harm them. In an attempt to protect themselves; they gave an offering to the gods and participants. Families would go door to door collecting food for the worshippers: TRICK OR TREAT. The pumpkins were carved and placed outside of homes to operate as a shield against the lost evil spirits that were believed to be released on earth. Costumes were worn by non-participants because the horrific costumes helped the townspeople blend in with the Satan worshipers so they would not be harmed. Catholic leaders of that time introduced the pagan holiday to the church making it a wide spread acceptable celebration. Celebrators had orgies and wild parties convinced they could celebrate Halloween and continue to be in the good graces of God. America's fore fathers opposed the holiday and left the celebration in the old world but in the late 1800s famine washed Irish Catholics onto America's shores and by the 1900s the celebration began to be accepted by Americans. Whether present day Americans want to face it or not Halloween is specifically for the celebration of Satan. Each year people go trick or treating, buy candy, have parties, decorate, host haunted houses, watch horror movies, wear (non)scary costumes, and throw raw eggs to celebrate a pagan holiday; a holiday based on fear. The celebrators are worshiping the devil. Steal, kill, and destroy is the agenda: Satan is not compassionate to people's consciousness or ignorance level of the pagan holiday. Celebrating is saying "yes Satan, I worship you." Every Oct. 31st our country is plagued with riots, destruction, and arson. Jesus can not protect us from the evil that Satan will rein on all who worship him. Holyween is no vindication. Children are still trick or treating and dressing up in costumes and evil is glorified through out most sacred blessings . . . our children.

The MAN is basically a white man who will do any and everything to profit and not concerned with who he hurts or what fundamental values are destroyed. If a white man can't have sex with it, eat it, or sell it, they kill it. Misconstrued holidays are more brilliant artful profitable systematic forms of the man. This misinformed society is held captive in his plots because of ignorance and conformity.

THE ROOT OF ALL EVIL

CHAPTER 10

The love of money is the root of all evil. As I review the past, look at the present, and try to foresee the future money has and will continue to be the underline cause of so much evil and corruption. This evil has spread beyond any race, religion, or culture; this evil is a world wide plague. People deceive, exploit, manipulate, back stab, and go against everything they believe in to increase the size of their pocket. Morals, values, integrity, family, friends, consequences, honesty, and character are over powered or are not of any importance. "By book or by crook," as long as the face of dead presidents printed on green sheets of paper is the reward. The world is under an evil spell that causes one to idolize money and materials. The spell can only be broken by surrendering the love we have to all worldly attachments. Under this spell, one is headed down a road filled with destruction and unsatisfaction is one of the many side effects. America has been under this spell since establishment and the sooner the American people realize that money is all she cares about the clearer things will become. Greed has a hold on our government and our leaders and politicians have been bought and America is in ruins.

North America was not discovered, people were already here with their own society, laws, and form of government and North America was their home. Christopher Columbus did stumble across America but by accident since he was going the wrong way. He was expecting to arrive in India explaining why Native Americans are ignorantly called Indians. After inspecting the land; Europeans saw how profitable the land could be and instead of fairly negotiating, Europeans began to kill the natives and forced them to reservations as if the land already belonged to them. With the new world conquered; Europeans sold the dream of indentured servants to the people of their land. Later the Europeans began to abduct Africans to work the land. Europeans bred the Africans like dogs, hoping to only produce physically strong slaves. Slaves ran away and fought for freedom and the Europeans began to take advantage of refugees and illegal aliens using them to build roads, bridges, railroads, buildings, and houses while paying little to nothing and reaping all profits. Those people built roads and bridges to separate them from non-white America; built buildings and homes only to set the criteria of who could enter; built new houses only for those who looked like white America and/or those who could afford the America dream. Founding fathers and those who followed in political power designed a government that would cater to their people. The justice system was corrupted from the beginning to ensure that harsh or appropriate punishment is given to non-white America while white America receives lenient or zero punishment. Money is even the reason for that. If nearly all of non-white America is in jail or illegal who are left to become active members of society?

Americans are more worried about outsiders working to bring down the U.S. ironically the outsiders are not who citizens should be worried about. America allows a countless number of illegal activities in exchange for dead presidents. In order for the government to pull of a successful scandal many people have to be paid off. Each and every one of those people paid off are the terrorist of this county. People do not sell secrets or turn on one another or this country for a trill; there is a price behind betrayal. Instead of troops invading other countries, America need honest investigators-if there is such a thing—to investigate and find America's own terrorist. Justice, honesty, and truth have been lost in the sea of money for a long time now.

Success:

One aspect of the American Dream teaches that a certain financial dollar has to be gained in order to be considered a success. Everyday people do things and face conditions they absolutely hate because the reward is not satisfaction and happiness but money. Money does not make a person successful but America teaches that because she is under the illusion that money can buy happiness. People work crazy hours, pursue dreams that others have for them, miss special irreplaceable moments, allow relationships and friendships to suffer, and make constant sacrifices to earn an increase in bank statements. But what is really America's definition of success? America defines success as the ability to obtain power, wealth, and worldly possessions. Not very often do we see a successful wealthy man who is happy or a successfully happy man who is wealthy. Many rich and wealthy are greedy and are always out to get more. America is filled with people who would casually leave the entire world poor as long as they are rich. Those people guilty but are God fearing; boggle my mind. How can one truly believe in God but idolize money and go against His Word for money to be rich on earth. America is the land of opportunity and success is obtainable; however, many become selfish and consumed with greed on the road to success-including the leaders of this country.

Compromise:

Television and movies are not pushing the envelope for the fun of it. The crazy and bizarre things seen on television are for ratings and ratings equal more money and the people in charge of networks and production for movies, television, and commercials receive healthy salaries. Actors and Actresses are not playing roles for an image and for the payout; and entertainers help America keep bias and stereotypical outlooks on race, religions, and gender. Television and movies also help moral less people build profitable businesses. Adultery on television are making companies billions of dollars. TV dramas portray married couples having affairs that are dressed up in gilt, glamour, and sexy love scenes. America has eaten up what is viewed and adultery has now become a trend. People have built corporations and websites based off the trend by making it easy to find other cheating spouses. The companies do not care about how many families are being destroyed and how many kids are losing their family and life as they know it to divorces. Does anyone care that this is plaguing the minds of children and young adults leaving them with compelled attitudes toward marriage.

Help me understand those who believe in God. Marriage is supposed to be a sacred oath in front of God, witnesses, and one another to fully commit; but spouses join websites that help to go against vows and betray the promise made to God. This behavior only hurts the upcoming generations because without marriage more and more kids will be born out of wedlock. Present day times show that the last the world needs is more shacking up and single parent homes. Marriage was put in place for a reason and it seems partners have no respect for themselves, their spouse, their families, and their promise made before God.

*Premarital sex adds to the abortion rate. Many babies have died as a result of women of all races and ages get pregnant and not want the children. Men and women are jointly deciding on the murder of innocent children to make their mistakes go away. 93% of women get abortions for social reasons; 47% have had at least one previous abortion. Race and religion are not important, focus on the aborted children. And lets remember all the medicine created that allows sexual activity without getting pregnant. That precaution basically constitutes premarital sex with teens because pregnancy is less likely to occur. 64.4% of abortions are by women who have never been married. If casual premarital sex stops the abortion rate could decrease 64.4%.

This cheating trend makes profit in more field than one. Divorce lawyers make their living off cheating and social websites and from the disrespect and disregard of partners. A divorce lawyer is unlikely to encourage clients to stay with spouses, suggest counseling, or any type of alternative instead of divorce. People are so sucked up into fantasy worlds and are failing to realize what is really happening. As long as profit is made and people are temporarily and superficially happy no one cares.

Compassion

Large corporations have no concern or compassion about the average person and their struggle especially if they are owed a debt. Debt is another way America controls her large credit holder population. The stock market crash reveals what America is really doing and how Americans are still in bondage. Credit card companies, debt consolidation, foreclosure, increase in daily products, and bankruptcy have brought Americans to their knees. Some are handling the disaster whit bizarre solutions. Suicide, murder, and theft have increased in number but THE MAN does not care. The IRS and debt collection companies have no thoughtfulness toward the people who pay the bills essential to their daily living; like mortgages, light bills, and car notes first. Companies abide by "don't ask don't tell" policies to put customers in nearly unbreakable contracts and keep them at a disadvantage, businesses have developed oblivious attitudes toward quality service and quality products. On top of all that; families are suffering stuck in a black hole not knowing which way is up, while companies aimed at greed buy the latest sports car. The "American Dream" misconception is the explanation of why some people are sucked up and drowned in debt. People are trying to buy things on credit that they cannot afford to appear to a certain standard to peers, family, and other social environments and wind-up worse than they were before. Society tells us that materials define who we are socially; people feed into it, then they get credit cards and loans to obtain items lusted for, ignoring the interest rated and the fact they can not afford the commitment required. This bubble keeps the rich rich and the poor poor. As long as Americans are in debt we are under the control THE MAN.

Everyday the world gets crueler and colder and many wonder why and how. The answer is money. Money makes society heartless and deceitful and the world will continue to spiral in a downward direction and we will eventually all destroy one another physically, emotionally, mentally, and finically. America lives by the motto "Nothing in life is free," because America puts a price on everything. When compromising ones self they have sold themselves. Guilt, physical and emotional pain, tears, lies, sacrifices, shame, worry, freedom, fear, punishable crimes, and eternal resting place are exchanged tender for money. At the end of the day Black or white are not the colors that matter GREEN is.

THE SYSTEM

CHAPTER 11

The system is flawed, but the system is corrupt because of the people. The structure of our government puts to much power in the hands of ordinary citizens. Local policeman can decide the fate of a person by a police report. Racism, stereotyping, and discriminative law holders file police reports and police documents based on their bias way of thinking. Police and court authorities have no consequences for their actions and take advantage of their power in our cities. Does the Judicial system teach integrity, loyalty, and honesty because a large percentage of officers and officials are corrupt and/or waiting on the highest bidder. Greed has the possession over so many of our law enforcement and leaders and our democratic system has been rigged since the days of establishment.

Police Corruption

Police and sheriff departments are measured, paid bonuses and raises, receiver promotions and commendations based on performance. Their performance is rated on the number of arrest and citations of either misdemeanors or felonies. Right or wrong crimes, citations, beyond reasonable doubt, and probable cause are not the reason reports are filed and are not what matter to officers. Arrests are important and police are filing false reports to further their career and fatten their pockets. In thorough reviews we would find false reports, false arrest, and innocent conviction by city police and sheriff departments in every state and with out media coverage they are getting away with it. Officers still use ignorance of the law against victims. With all these reasonless arrest it leaves me to wonder how many of the 13 to 15 million arrested a year are innocent and who is law enforcement targeting. (Black men are a large percentage) Minorities are the main targets because the court system will take the word of an officer over civilians. Police are human and capable of mistakes, errors, and lies yet in court they are automatically right without question or investigation. People are fined, prosecuted, and found guilty, and officers are deliberately making false claims. Even though officers use their own reasoning with civilians does not always make them reasonable people. Every kind, color, religion, and ethnic group commits crimes and statistics are not enough for me; and probable cause is not always so probable. Just because statistics say that certain people who fit into certain categories are more prone to commit certain crimes does not make it ok for officers to harass and arrest those stereotypes. How can America expect Americans to trust law enforcement?

The Black Market

The success level of the system can not increase because the police corruption affects it. Law enforcement officers live and ride our city streets keeping the "animals" off the streets and are "protecting and serving" the people of the area; yet the animals are wearing the badges. To many of our law enforcers are corrupt and some are as criminal and corrupt as they come. The truth behind the filthy badges is drugs. No organized crime can run without the help of the justice and court systems. Society, television, and movies portray drug dealers as some of the worse people. Where do you think the drugs come from? How do drug dealers keep getting away with all the illegal activity? The government makes a lot of money from drugs. Drugs are sold on the black market and is a multi-million dollar industry in the U.S. and a billion dollar industry globally. Drug dealers are thugs on the street terrorizing neighborhoods and its inhabitants. Yeah right. Drugs are the number one cause of police corruption. This profitable industry can not and will not exist without the help of law enforcement and law makers locally and nationally. Police are 1. conducting unconstitutional searches and seizures; 2 stealing money and/or drugs from drug dealers; 3 selling stolen drugs; 4 protecting drug operations; 5 providing false testimony; and 6 submitting false crime reports. Drug dealing is a business and since it is illegal it attracts devious, dishonest, disloyal, questionable shady participants. Badges, uniforms, and labels do not change the person; hell the badges, uniforms, labels, and rank are used to commit countless crimes escaping without question. Did Americans believe the only drug dealers were predominantly Black males? Drug dealers come in different shapes, sizes, and colors; cars with rims are the least of America's worries.

Delusions=Errors

America's court system bring down harsh punishments on the dealers as if they are the scum of the earth. America has a wonderful outlook on things. Pedophiles and rapist are the terrorist. Child molesters sexually abuse innocent children and leave them torn, hurt, confused, misguided, afflicted the rest of their life and agonized with dreadful memories that could alter their future drastically. Men and women are engaging in illegal activity and mentally, physically, and emotionally hurt unwilling participants. Children are my biggest issue. Children are the future and America does not care about their emotional state or how well they will function in society. Women that care for their families have been burdened with rape and many of their predators have not been caught. Rapists affect millions of people directly and indirectly. Some rapist murder or leave victims afraid for the rest of their life. Prison, spousal, gang, and date are different areas of rape and sexual assault. Statistics try and predict rapes and sexual assaults of the future and try to calculate the rape and sexual abuse that is not reported. Force, power, violence, and fear are weapons used against victims for rapist's orgasm, sick pleasures, twisted fantasies, and unheard of fetishes and this country is infested with hundreds of thousands sick souls. There are about 400,000 REGISTERED sex offenders with 80 to 100,000 missing. The average child molester receives 11 years but 77.9% are out of jail within 2 years. Rapist and sex offenders get short sentences then get released back into society by the justice system only having to register in the neighborhood they reside leaving parents afraid to let their children play outside. Instead of our law enforcement looking and watching for pedophiles and rapist; they are preoccupied profiling, harassing, and searching for drug dealers. Drug dealers are bad but at least they are not forcing the drugs on addicts. Drugs in America are illegal but society administers harsher punishments on pharmacist than rapist, pedophiles, and sometime murders. Restaurants feed peoples eating addictions and liquor stores feed alcohol addiction both can be as deadly as drugs.

The Nature of the Beast

"Rape is apart of a culture of violence and an expression of the male dominance. (Sandy 1979). The male ego will drive him to extreme measures to insure that he dominate the situation and the person(s) in it. Rape is a male proclaiming dominance over a women proves to the attacker that he is in control and no matter if she says no, no matter if her privacy is invaded, and no matter if she violated sexually and physically because the attacker is only concerned with his own selfish desires that drive him to rape no matter what actually drives the rapist. This strokes the "male ego of dominance" and the male walks away feeling like "he did something." I condone the theory that the culture of society and social structure contribute to the violent sexual crime. Images and music through media also play a role by making rape look interesting, entertaining, and implies satisfaction in movies, television, and video games; while also promoting sex through music, television, movies, and video games.

Males are considered to be the king of the jungle. The lion-male-feel he owns and controls that entire territory-women—when he chooses. Why? 1. He has an ego and a society and social structure that still say that women are inferior to men. Ex. Explains why women had to fight to be treated equally and not be cut out of all the roles of power. Ex. Examine how the middle east treats their women and how the US have to carefully watch the position that military women are put in due to the extreme culture difference of the roles and social structure of those people. 3. The male has physical power to eat any animal-have sex with any women—whether the animal wants to be eaten or not. It is the nature of the beast.

Violent sexual crimes are wrong due to the fact, that despite the fact that men are acting like animals, the men are human beings who have a self. They posses the ability to associate symbols and emotions together and can choose the basis of how they act, the ability to judge the situation and understand the difference of good and bad, understand the general respect that should be given to a women no matter her weakness and vulnerability, and to understand themselves better as men-individually—and learn how to control sexual impulses that maybe feed by media while also figuring out a way to deal with anger, sadness etc.

Men who rape girlfriends and spouses may stem from anger, stress, frustration, pressure, or sadness but what is constant no matter the reason is that man has marked that women as his territory and she belongs to him *especially married couples. This in his mind gives him the authority to do what he pleases. The continuation of the rape in relationships is "just because I "forcefully" had sex with my wife, we still engaged in consensual sexual acts. That fact is eluding the man to think that it is ok despite the pain he causes by his actions.

(Blumberg 1979) "In pre-industrial societies women are more likely to lack important life options and to be physically

and politically oppressed where they lack economic power relative to men." Since we are human beings with a self and a need for a society and social structure—due to the complexity of our anatomy—those same animalistic qualities are carried out in our society and the ability and power to repress the weaker race-women—is the male ego. Dominance= Power. It is widely agreed that rape is a tactic used by men to insure social control. Social control= Power= Dominance.

The social control is also feed by the influence, folkways, and mores, rules, and regulations of society. Men are naturally the lion while also written through out Western history and majority cultures that men are the head of the house hold and their job is to take care of the women and children. If a man does not or can not do that society judges and labels him as "less than a man." The feminist of rape 1775 view "rape as an act of violence and social control which functions to "keep women in their place." "Extension of normative male behavior, the result of conformity or over conformity to the values and prerogatives which define the traditional male role" but as a result have contradictive beliefs that have both been embedded into society. Men are supposed to take care of the women but not allowed to be pleased by the women they choose to be with. As for rapists without partners—they are driven by sexual impulse, the amount of sex that comes in television, movies, and advertisement, and the emotional build up because society judges and labels teaching that Emotions= Weakness, Sensitivity = Weakness, and the bias outlook society has between women and men and the double standard for sexual history.

(Bart 1979) "This justification for forced sexual access is buttressed by legal, social and religious definitions of women as male property and sex as an exchange of goods." Sex as an exchange for goods has been prevalent through out history; nonetheless that does not equal rape. Majority rape victims

are not prostitutes and do not receive anything tangible from a rape attack. Community rapes are stimulated around ego and casual relationships. Most rapist—whether married or not—are serial rapist and women appear vulnerable, kindness is taken for weakness, and men take advantage. The violence of these crimes erupt because women say no and try to fight or resist the rape—although the violence is sometimes what turns on the rapist. The king of the jungle dominates the territory-the woman—and devours her. How by having complete control and by disabling her physical abilities to fight back—sometimes resulting in murder.

"Images projected in pornography contribute to a vocabulary of motive which trivializes and neutralizes rape and which might lessen the internal controls that otherwise would prevent sexually aggressive behavior." Pornography itself stimulates the arousal in the brain to want to commit a sexual act not necessarily saying that it has to be a violent one. The extremeness of pornography and the ability to watch any type of porn-whether it be sick or not—is what drives a person to commit more brutal rapes. Even television and movies show rough sexual acts and the women appear to be enjoying themselves and that feeds the theory that "if I do this to a woman she will like it." This also creates imagination and fantasy; which deepen the mental arousal and begins to appear in the day dreaming and thought process. This lion-the man—is now on the prow. He begins to move quiet and undetected until he moves in on his territory. Married rapist wives are marked as "constant territory." Rapist—no matter the victim or the level of violence—feels they can justify the rape—no matter how brutal or deadly—because the woman had an orgasm or she begins to enjoy it. Rapists ignorantly ignore the violence, the violations, and the forced penetration by focusing on the fact that the victim had an orgasm(s). "If rape is so wrong why did

I watch media and porn that glamorized this act?" "And why no matter how much pain she says she was in and no matter how traumatic did she still orgasm?"

The contradictions of beliefs have resulted in individual and society based chaos. The human body is created with the ability to receive pleasure. Despite the emotional and physical pain the body maybe receiving, the brain also receives signals from the body that read "pleasure." Orgasms are the way the body enjoys the pleasure and how it releases it. Rapists misconstrue that observation. They think the women enjoyed it and feel proud withstanding the harness act and the inflicted pain on the victim. How do they feel good? Their ego and hunger for dominance is fed, they receive pleasure, gave the victim pleasure as far as they can see, and/or feel the victim deserved what they got. The rapist ability to make the victim orgasm is no different than a married man making love to his wife and making her orgasm. In the rapist mind "you had an orgasm; so what are you complaining about?" "You know you liked it so what are you complaining about?"

Rape is psychological but heavily influenced by society. Even convicted rapists who are "habilitated" are only "cured" for so long—hence why law enforcements wait on offenders to mess up. Those same images, sounds, and symbols that influenced the rapist in the beginning, continue to surround him. Homosexuality, rape in prison, television, movies, and music are there to face a convicted rapist in prison and wait on him at the gate when he leaves.

Society's molestation, overexposure, misinformation, and religious beliefs drive rape and rape victims. Mutual respect, understanding, controlled sexual desires, control of the sexual content and contexts in any and all TV. magazines, movies, music, and advertisement, and reducing the casualties of sex could help in preventing curious premature sexual acts. Teaching and learning how to constructively release the emotions of stress, sadness, anger, revenge, and frustration may help as well.

Anger and revenge drive some rapist. Why? That individual does not feel that they are in the power position. Whether it is a wife, girlfriend, or random woman or whether the victim is personally involved with the emotion problem(s) the rapist has; those repressed emotions make him feel like he is "losing" and some how he has to win because he has to feed his hunger for dominance in order to feed his ego. As a result he preys on a weaker predator not matter if it is viewed as right or wrong. This can also be a point of contradictive beliefs because society teaches men that Emotions = Weakness. That man does not want to be labeled or judged by society so he lives without expressing intimate thoughts, feelings, fears, worries, and emotional pain. The energy from emotions is repressed over time-time may vary—and the men become so enraged that they have to release it. (Crying could sometimes help but is shunned by society) The rape is not positive and is illegal but it releases stress, anger, and revenge, while continuing to feed the role of being dominant. Especially in instances for men who gang rape or date rape with deception and drugs. The men congratulate each other and stroke one another's ego while also making one another feel accepted.

The contrary to the men are the women. Women are often victims of rape but also play a role in the effects. Sex on television by women actresses help in the men's fantasizing. The entertainment will always find someone who is willing to play roles; but the more extreme the visuals are, the more poisons of validation for the man is stimulated. Pornography and the contents go beyond insinuations and provide visual satisfaction for the men. Access to underage porn and monster porn is another topic in itself, nonetheless creates more issues in the matter. The influence, freedom, and assorted articles of *clothing give women the option to look like prostitutes, business women, urban etc, but revealing clothes put the opportunity of rape in arms reach. Revealing clothes is NOT the reason men rape, nonetheless that may give him validation in touching or for thoughts to attempt rape. Men think "why would she dress like that if she didn't want the attention?" Attention being looking, touching, and even rape.*

What could women do to prevent rape is a question that can not be answered due to the various yet obvious reasons that men rape to begin with. Society has deep roots in this matter and it probably dates back to ancient times, meaning no couple of people can effectively change the presence of rape in society anytime soon. Women have to just be careful in their actions and words in dealing with guys that they "know," think they "know," do not "know," or thought they "knew," and not put themselves in vulnerable positions.

Married women may have to do individual and couple counseling to figure out the points of frustration, anger, and sadness to balance their repressed emotions and express them in a positive manner vs. rape. The display of love could keep help by the wife showing the man that he will always be "the man" in her eyes and she accepts him no matter people or society. Most importantly the man must admit he has problems/troubles and be willing to look at themselves in the mirror in their true reality.

Women also contribute to rape by promiscuous behavior and the leading on of men. Women will walk and talk sex but are only joking with the idea but not realizing that she could be feeding a fantasy in the mans brain. Implications and flirty conversations lead men to think that they have the "ok" to make a move. Some women tease men intently; thinking that her actions are not taken serious by the male. Women who have no intentions on having sexual contact with should refrain from sexual conversations and flirty acts. Women sometimes become rape victims by misinterpretations on both sides. Women do not take their words and actions serious while the man is reading the words and actions that encourage him to make a move that sometimes ends in rape. In addition to flirty behavior women nowadays get so intoxicated in public settings and present themselves more vulnerable. Men take advantage of the opportunity and do not care if the women pass out during sex. Men intentionally go out and pay these women "special" attention. Women have to be careful.

Penalties

Police and courts look at the weight, type of drug, and prior convictions in deciding on arrest and sentencing. 5 to 10 years is the average sentence that dealers receive and the "Good Behavior" promise actually give prisoners only 54 days per year off their sentence; requiring them to serve 85% of their sentence. In 1986 the average federal drug sentence for Blacks was 11% higher than whites and four years later the average drug federal sentence for Blacks was 49% higher. Drugs and police corruption explain the prison over crowd. Seeing that America has not shed far away from her racist tactics; I'm certain the average federal drug sentence for Blacks remain higher than whites. Guess my community finally beat whites at something . . . conviction rates. Many drug dealers commit non-violent crimes yet America trails them like murders when the local, federal, and national government are providing them with the drugs. Isn't the "American" Justice System just great!? ***Especially for African Americans***

Insight

On many occasions the Black community is driven to a life of crime and hustling. White people have made the success ladder harder to climb for Blacks, specifically for the men. Society begins by telling the Black community they will never amount to anything, they foresee the future for Black men as either dead or in jail by 21, and make the outlets sports, entertainment, politics, or military. With limited jobs our community has become poor and in a tough economical position because bills do not stop coming and we all have to eat. Society feeds us all this "America Dream" fascination and BAM!! Robbing and stealing sky rocket in the Black community. The Black community has a choice not to commit crimes and/or hustle; yet hard when a quick hustle is always in arms reach. "Get it how you live," is the motto of so many Blacks in the world struggling. Citizens go to work for minimum wage, uncle Sam and the state take their cut, and leave part time workers with very little. "All this clocking in and out for nothing; hell I could have robbed someone and the same $200 I worked for 2wks in 2 minutes" is a thought of Blacks or anyone who is really struggling. Crime in America is odd though: 1. How did Blacks begin to target one another instead of the real thief? 2. How did Blacks become burdened with the stealing stereotype? People have been stealing since the beginning of time and color has nothing to do with it. America does not seem to quite understand the EVERYONE IN AMERICA is capable of crime. America was founded on unquestionable illegal acts and murder. America still robs Blacks of our rightful position in society, our earned promotions, our right to live where ever we choose without being treated unequally, our right for Black men to drive wherever they want without being racially profiled, and our right to be on an equal scale as whites. The bailout gave us an insightful look at who the real knifings thieves were. White-collar crimes are still crimes! Blue-collar crimes and misdemeanors typically affect people on a much smaller scale than white collar crimes; unsurprisingly blue-collar offenders are trailed and punished much harsher than white collar offenders. Since Black people are taboo in the white-collar work place; who are left to commit the white-collar crime? America has used stereotyping to cover up the money hungry thieves.

These 7 suggestions have been reported to possibly effectively lower crime rate:

- Put More Police on the Street
- Put More Criminals in Prison.
- Focus on Habitual Criminals
- Keep Violent Criminals in Prison Longer.
- Focus National and State Resources on Criminals, Not Weapons
- Provide Alternative Sentencing for Non-Violent Offenders
- Develop Community Programs Which Deter Crime

5 suggestions of my own:

- More police would possibly lead to more police corruption
- The prisons are already over crowded and many are innocent or over sentenced
- The justice system is shady and shallow

- Nobody wants to take the time to think of alternative methods. Few people care and white collar crimes give the true corrupters and criminals a slap on the wrist
- People want to keep funds in their pocket so who will support these community programs

Oath

"Do you swear to tell the truth, the whole truth, and nothing but the truth?" Court participants and witnesses inevitably respond "yes" to this question with their right hand on the Bible and flat-out lie on the stand. Many people testify with the intent to lie and deceive other court parties. How can/will there be justice for all if cases are opened and closed based on lies. Attorneys manipulate and intimidate witnesses, jurors, and on lookers for a win. Justice and the right to a fair trail do not exist in our courts; the system is the system and participants maneuver around laws and clauses to make it work in their favor. America's justice and court system is defective and our government and the people who run it preach what is not practiced.

COMMANDER AND CHIEF

CHAPTER 12

Fans of George W. Bush are numbered and the reasons are justifiable. Many Americans are opposed to Obama but much of the dislike began the first time citizens saw and heard his campaign. A nigger running for president is simply unheard of in the mind of so many Americans. Some racist who would, could, or did any and everything humanly possible to prevent such a historical and long awaited event from happening. Streams of negativity surround one man through negative comments, stories, publicity, and rumors filling the headlines and news reports. Is he not a U.S. citizen? Is this not the land of the free and land of opportunity? Had he not taken the necessary steps and met the criteria to qualify for such a high-ranking government position? After the circulation of rumors questioning his citizenship; he provided his birth certificate but the thanks goes to the mistakes of former President Bush and his 2nd election. Obama won the title of Commander and Chief of the United States of America because the entire country was at wits end and McCain campaign was Dr. King running against Hitler. "The People" got what they asked for: Barack Obama; but he is hounded and questioned with whom, what, when, where, and how and in doing so Americans are confessing "yes" voted to elect him but "no" we do not trust his judgment. Why vote for someone if they will only receive criticism, ridicule, and bad publicity from the people who put them in office? On the other hand; when our dear Bush made absurd, brainless, foolish, reasonless decisions there were no protesters or bodies of people wishing failure upon him. Americans played follow the leader no matter how much of an idiot the leader may have been.

Election mudslinging paints a picture of who politicians are and how far and/or low they will go to have their way. Americans can not deny that though out Obama's entire campaign he did not allow his desire to win change who he was and within 24 hours after his win; Americans proceeded to beat down his door with complaints and expectations. Although Bush is responsible for the majority of the economic problems; everyone is still looking at Obama as if he single-handedly caused the economic and education crisis.

Where was the violent town hall meeting over the "War on Terrorism?" And America's congress agreed on the war. Our soldiers were deployed to look for a man who may or may not have committed terrorism against our country. Our men and women fought, died, and were wounded in a war created by an unfit president. 911 showed the extremes of our government and the stock market crash unveiled tactics of the government to cheat and deceive the American people. Nobody held Bush, congress, or Wall Street accountable and by the time people realized what had happened it was too late. Things were so damaged it would take years to fix and Bush's 2nd term was up. While

Americans were trying to figure out what to do and how it all happened; Bush was a lame duck. The Bush administration were crooks and all the attacks and threats to America was carefully planned and thought out. Wars, unfortunate events, and propaganda hide the truth and motives behind the fall of America. It seems like nobody cared what Bush did; he served 2 terms. The government has lead its people down a road of deception, then ceased any evidence of the truth; which has left Americans terrified and lost. America knew Bush was an idiot by the end of the first term yet he was reelected with a tract record with not one good idea. Special exceptions and compromises were made to bring Bush into office and voters gave bush a 2nd term and had to sit and watch the disasters that followed that ballet.

Americans call Barack Obama a liar and act as if he should have super powers to fix the mess that America has found herself in. Obama has one of the hardest jobs in this county; he has to be the figure face for the rise and fall of this country whether he is responsible or not. *"Since it was a miracle he was elected, he needs to be a miracle worker."* A lot of the negativity and anger originated because of his skin tone despite his white mother. Most Americans say he is Black because Black is the dominant color of his skin; but honestly he is not Black. Had his dominant color been white America would have called him white and all the hoopla would not exist. If Obama was white, America would blame Bush because the new "white" president was not apart of the Bush Administration; but Obama is Black so America blame and ridicule him. That is generally how it works in America: BLAME THE BLACK MAN *especially if he is angry. Obama's has been scrutinized under a microscope since the day of inauguration. Not only are they carefully reviewing every bill, document, and proposal; they are even reviewing his underwear drawer. Everybody is trying to find something bad to say about him and of course there is always plenty to say bad about anyone.

Through my eyes:

This is no democracy and sovereignty is just talk. White men who do not hold the public spot light run this country and despite all the uproar over the 2008 presidential election, Obama was expected to win because the government organized it. The government plans to use him to their advantage. Obama as president is a skim for the American people to begin to put trust in government again and after trust is obtained the government is going to deceive and kill again. Obama is the figure face of the American government, meaning when things go sour the entire country will blame him and drag him though the media worse than before and all the true culprits will be unseen and unknown. The same may have occurred with George W. Bush. After listening to him speak; it did not take rocket science to know he was an idiot and the unseen used that as an advantage. Hard to believe all of his decisions that resulted in mistakes were accidents. He served 2 terms and won the merit of one the worse presidents in history. Honest men work hard to not obtain such a title.

THE UNWRITTEN RULES

CHAPTER 13

Despite the history of Africans Americans in the 21st century the use of the word Nigga continues to be utilized. Americans wonder is there a difference in "Nigger" and "Nigga?" Here is understanding and/or an answer:

Nigger is a word used to degrade and belittle Blacks dating before slavery and now. Nigger was derived from the Spanish and there word for the color Black. Whites in that time used Nigger as disrespect. Blacks were called insulting adjectives because of color, literacy, intelligence, economical status, social status, and as a way for whites to feel superior to Blacks. Slavery may be long gone but much of white America feel that Blacks are still a bunch of savages ruining the country. When the Black community say Nigga; they are using in a socially acceptable manner intending no harm, disrespect, or insult any ones intelligence, economical status, social status, or literacy. Nigga is just another word as if saying friend, man, or referring to a person meaning no disrespect even if they are not Black. The ending of Nigger—er has been changed and substituted with—a.

Although my community uses the word; some Blacks feel the word needs to cease and desist feeling the word still degrades African Americans, while other Blacks feel the word has had its run and it is time to give it a rest. The first amendment allows the usage of both words—Nigger and Nigga—making it virtually impossible to dictate and history has embedded that word in the heart of America.

The real question is how much of white America still see Blacks as Niggers? Being unable to answer this question is why Blacks are still angered when whites use the word. Most whites use the word to express their racial feelings and thoughts with the intent to hurt and insult. Most times those people do not use the word publicly or at all; nonetheless African Americans are still being measured and negatively labeled as less than by attitudes related to the word. Blacks use Nigga from daily conversations to hip-hop lyrics. It remains a problem to those who think it keeps our race from progessing and those who believe it is disrespectful to call one another by a word that has held African Americans "down" for so long.

Words are very powerful and have the ability to tear done as well as build up. The word Nigga has matured by changing the spelling and has evolved in definition by broadening the meaning. With that being said; if the Black community can come to an agreement and understanding about the word what is the problem? Nigga is no different than the usage of bitch or hoe among people who do not take offense to the word. Nigger is no different from a foe using bitch or hoe intending to hurt or degrade. I'm personally offended when whites use Nigger because racism, bias thinking, and discrimination hurt my community; however it does not bother me when whites use Nigga. If the thought process changes, then so does the meaning of a word. The word is not the root of the problem it is what comes to mind when one hears it and the word does not hurt; it is the intention behind the word. The word Nigger has and always will have bad intentions; nonetheless, Nigga will not hurt or degrade.

Whites also treat my community like Niggers. If you think I am dumb and treat me like a dummy then; you may as well call me a dummy. Same with Nigger. If you think a young Black male is a Nigger; regardless of if you verbally say it, you will treat him according to what your definition of Nigger is. Once again it is not the word now it is the action and Actions speak louder than words.

Blacks took a word that was used against them, changed the ending, and made it acceptable among themselves shows positive development in the Black community. America has a habit of focusing the wrong thing to hide the real problems. Society is worried about Blacks calling one another Niggas, but neglects that whites still refer and treat my community like Niggers. Those of the Black community who feel the reconstruction of the word holds our community down, I ask: How can a word hold a race of people down? That is an excuse. What is REALLY holding the Black community down and back is THE BLACK community.

NO MORE

Frequently Blacks can joke and make fun of whites who typically do or say nothing but when the situation is reversed there is a confrontation. Not only is society afraid of Blacks but Blacks young, old, male or female are afraid of Blacks; especially Black men. People often wonder why Blacks are so angry and belligerent; Reasons may vary, some look at the crime rate, some look at dress, actions, and speech. The truth is the Black community has become prejudice to one another and is making a subconscious choice to be this way; the most important part to an understanding is the role history plays.

Slavery has been over for decades yet after slavery Blacks were spit on, beat, made fun of, lied on, mistreated, used, cheated, and locked out of society. Blacks grew tired and created a new unwritten rule "don't take no shit from white folks." Then Blacks began to treat one another like whites treated Blacks and the unwritten rule became "don't take no shit from NOBODY." My community carries this attitude on their shoulder with no hesitation to display it. Ultimately as a community, Blacks do take white folks shit in some shape, form, or fashion because white folks still act like masters and we Black folk have to follow their every command. Can one now understand the complexity of our anger? Our Black men are under the most stress; Black men attempt the straight and narrow path but faced with the reality that America really wants them to fail. My community of men has a choice: Work twice as hard as white America just too constantly be fucked over one way or another or go astray. Many of you would say work twice as hard; I say, why should they have to work twice as had if this is the land of equality with equal opportunity?

Nonexistence

America tricks people to believe in things that do not exist. Fictional cartoon, dramas, and movies are built on murderous evil demons, aliens, goblins, vampires, monsters, supernatural humans, and supernatural creatures. Americans young and old begin to believe these things exist and that they may become a victim if they are not careful. This fear makes people paranoid and afraid of what is not really there. Americans who allow themselves to be consumed with fear and believe in fiction are probably the same who believe media gossip, the daily news, peers, daily conversations and family. Television broadcast movies and drama series with ordinary people with special powers who fight the evil demons; drama series with the daily life of the evil; reality shows showing people chasing ghost and spirits; drama series that show people falling in love with supernatural creatures; movies display extreme possible outcomes of serial murders, unordinary deaths, creatures rising from the dead, immortal supernatural evil aliens, possessed animals, insects, ghost, goblins, and creating extraordinary end of the world outcomes; movies and television are directed with the primary intent to scare. The viewing of these shows effect our thinking process over any period of time and the enjoyment of these shows and movies are scheduled around our days. Networks even create children television series and movies with fairies, genies, wizards, witches, ghost, goblins, and monsters. American children are afraid without night lights and/or sleeping with one another/ parents to feel safe because of images seen on television. America begins to imbed senseless fears and paranoia's in society at young ages slightly shifting the foundation of the mind; and children group believing what is seen and heard on televisions, movies, news, magazines, and the internet; then the media begins to feed to children and adolescents illusions of all kinds. Reality is compromised and day dreams are reenacted; rated R movies target an older generation and the fear and paranoia continue to be imbedded in our upcoming generations. Gossip magazines, internet social networks and blogs, television and movies, and fabricated news reports continue to mislead the truth and replace it with lies and fairy tales. Propaganda in the media twists the thought process of all who believe it and the separation lines and history remains in place. Due to the foundation of fear; people cling to their appearance and acceptance groups are prejudice to the people who do not fit; and the media decides what is in and what is out. Men and women in society of all ages long for what is seen on television; despite the truth that everyone can not look like the glamorized beauties of media, society criticizes all who do not resemble it. Exterior appearance and attire are weighed heavily against those who are different; foreigners are criticized the most for arriving in America with established cutomes and way of life that not always resemble America's way of life. American families are responsible in the teaching of beliefs, values, and mores and most of America's children learn color, nationality, and culture make a difference in the treatment of individuals; look more at the negative and differences in one another; are unwilling to give one another a chance; and are living though the opinions of other people. Domestication of this sort creates more needless fear, more social boundaries, and more preconceived notations.

The Cycle

People tend to believe everything they hear as if people do not lie. It is not until gossip and lies affect Americans personally that they do not want people to believe the nonsense and gossip being said. Basically: "Everything a person hears and says is true until they are ones being talked about." Most of things people discuss on a daily basis are based on someone else's experience and people tend to tell a story the way they want it to be heard even if there is little to no truth in it; thus creating a body of lies and stereotypes leaving a social hole between Americans. It is as if Americans have been brainwashed. There are hardly any free thinkers; there are no true believers; judgments can easily be swayed; everyone is so easily influenced and quick to conform. Everyone is seeking approval from society or his or her social environment turning us into hamsters on a spinning wheel.

WE DID IT TO OURSELVES

AM I NOT A MAN AND A BROTHER?

WHO'S TO BLAME?

Finger pointing has never been good unless one is willing to acknowledge their own faults and take responsibility for their own actions. No matter what whites have done, Blacks have played an active role in the rise and fall of our community. Blacks have made keeping us under social control easy and we contribute greatly to the rut of our community. There is always that "shoulda, woulda, coulda" nonsense; but that is said when it is over. What is being said while it is happening? Nothing. The history of our ancestors cannot be changed, however the recent past and present will become the future if the Black community does not wake up and realize the faults and mistakes that are causing failure. Responsibility for actions has not been taken in a long time and Blacks no longer strive to make Black America better. Marches, movements, protest, sit-ins, strikes, pititions, and great leaders have done the hardest parts. Now in the 21st century our community can not even graduate from school. Our community does not take pride in who we are and no longer work to become the best individually or as a community to break down the remaining barriers. The focus of our community has been on what the white people are doing to keep us down instead of what we are not doing to come up. A cloud of shame hovers over our community and we confirm the awful stereotypes continuously with disgraceful, naïve, mindless, poor, negligent behavior. Our communities remain in poor conditions socially and economically; we have given up on our community; Black families are no longer pushing our kids to their true potential; there are not enough positive role models on television or at home to show children and young adults the right way; and our men are falling in the same never-ending cycle generation after generation. When will our community finally be held to a higher standard? I'll tell you: when people stop making excuses for bad behavior; when people grow; when men and women take responsibility in raising our children; when people believe in themselves; when people see their life and the state of their life with glasses of truth and judge THEMSELVES honestly.

**Those people = White people

-Determined to do
The only thing you could do
Determined to save
The only life you could save.
The Journey
Mary Oliver

FEBUARY

Black history month is the month of February, which is the shortest month of the year. I always thought it was because white folks wanted it to be that way but it turns out that February has been an important month for us through out history.

- Feb. 23, 1868, W. E. B. Dubois founder of the NAACP was born.
- Feb 3, 1870: The 15 amendment was passed granting Blacks the right to vote.
- Feb 25, 1870: First Black U.S. Senator, Hiram R. Revels, took his oath in office.
- Feb 1, 1960: 1st milestone of the Civil Rights Movement, college students did a sit-in at a lunch counter.
- Feb 21, 1963: Malcolm X was shot to death.
- Feb 2nd: Eric H. Holder Jr. voted first Black to serve as attorney General.

These are just a few dates in history but there are many more historical facts about our past that and I encourage everyone to research.

FORESEEN AS . . .

CHAPTER 14

In the eyes of some white people, Blacks are still savages.
Savage: 1. Not civilized; primitive. 2. Not tamed; fierce; wild. 3. Cruel brutal man—a person living in a primitive or uncivilized way.

Niggers are a bunch of lazy belligerent excuses for man and prone to committing crimes. What were they thinking when they brought Africans to this country??

The Europeans observed, interacted, traded, and noted the Africans on paper before either of them began to settle in America. Africans and Blacks were never savages; they were a different type of people with a different way of life. If anyone wants to argue and say that Africans were savages; I will agree, under the consideration of how Africans arrived on North American soil and how they were treated as such. On the ride over Africans were chained like dogs; and after arrival breed, beat, traded, and sold like animals.

Many white/Europeans described slaves to be inferior to whites, weak minded, unfit to gain success, stupid people who lacked courage. Stupidity was held to be true; true only on the condition that whites made slaves that way. Ignorance was the main component in keeping the control. If a man knows nothing he can accomplish nothing. Slaves were taught only how to complete the job they occupied. Whites felt slaves were inferior and weak minded because slaves allowed themselves to be entrapped and remain in the devastating state for hundreds of years. Where slave not courageous because they never rebelled? Well; anyone caught trying to help slaves organize was considered to be committing treason; slaves were slaughtered at every attempt to rebel; and all slaves were not quite ready to pay the price of freedom. No matter the case; every adjective used in describing slaves, whites can be given the credit seeing that they contributed greatly in sculpting the image of slaves. Proslavery felt that the slaves were content and the abolitionist teachings were the cause of the discontent ness. Honestly some slaves were content with the slave status because although slavery in general was wrong, not all slaves were treated badly. Abolitionist teaching had little to do with slave's attitude toward slavery. And if slaves were so "content" why did they run away; why did they poison the masters and family; why did free Blacks eventually out number slaves? My point exactly: Blacks desired not to be slaves. Whites could clearly see Blacks urge for freedom; however, to impart independence with Blacks was felt to be dangerous. Were whites afraid of real equality? A Black possibly surpassing them was the fear. Slaves may have not been taught much; nonetheless, that did mean slaves were incapable of learning. A person's mental capacity has no relation to color and free slaves were showing America that they were able to live and maintain free from the rule of a master. Had Blacks not been in bondage long enough? Slaves survived 400 years under the rule of another man differing only in color and after being forced to this country Blacks have rightfully earned their place in a fair society. We never asked for the boat ride over here so who must the Black community continue to suffer because whites/Europeans decided to enslave a group of people.

PUBLIC SERVICE ANNOUCEMENT: Majority of whites still feel that Blacks are inferior to whites, weak minded, unfit to gain success, and content in poverty.

From the outside looking in it would appear to be true. The truth is that our community is just LAZY!! Our minds are not weak; they are just filled with unrealistic realities; Success is obtainable, many just are not willing to put in the time and energy it takes to succeed; And of course some are content with their economical status due to the assistance of the government. These are the true realities of our community so either you are apart of the problem or part of the solution.

Everyone is trying so hard to shy away from the way Blacks are stereotyped and I have a problem with that. No matter who you are or what you are doing in life it still does not change the fact that you are Black! I see no need to convince America that we are above everything she says about us but rather see to need to better ourselves individually and not fall into the trap America has set. Blacks have to achieve personal goals and become who we want to be in life. I see nothing wrong with an intelligent Black but Blacks' change who they are in whites presence.

I am all for elaborate vocabularies, intellectual conversations, exceptional educations, and fancy lifestyles; except when everything one does is to try and prove that you can be just as white or as good a person as they are, we are 1. Admitting we think they are better 2. showing that they actually do have social control over us. White people want to dress, talk, and act Black but do not want to be called a nigger, let alone be treated like one. They act like us for the fun of it but we act like them for approval from society.

CONTROL

CHAPTER 15

We, Black people, give white people control. We allow their views, opinions, culture, and lifestyle to dictate our lives, views, opinion, and lifestyle. Here in MS, Black people say things like: You better stop, see all these white people/I was bout to ____ but it was too many white folks/Act like you got some sense in front of these white folks/ I was ____ but had to stop because white folks started looking at me crazy. Why does their presence matter so much and I doubt those people change or refrain because of Black folks. Whites may lock car doors, clench purses, and make sure they have their keys in hand before arriving at their car, but other than that they act however they choose.

NONE OF US WILL EVER BE GOOD ENOUGH in the majority of those people eyes so why are we seeking their approval? White people are treated, decided and held upon the material things they possess. They have their expensive brand of everything and when they have or can obtain a large percentage of expensive things they gain the status of living the "American Dream."—which is perfectly fine for them but not for the Black community. Trying to live the American Dream is the one reason the Black community is in ruins in addition to buying the equality lie! We will not be equal until we all look alike—no matter what we buy; even when richer the equality problem still exist.

Face that Blacks are different from whites. Social control: If we are working to become like them then they control us. At the end of the day it will *never* be enough because they keep changing the criteria. First it was learn to read, then it was learn to how to write, then it was something else to keep us out. Our community is under the illusion that expensive materials determine who you are and how to be treated. That is a lie and we need to leave that simple-minded nonsense to those people. People of color get self absorbed and think they are bettering themselves and life by furnishing their life with modern technology and latest fashion; but the interior growth is delayed and problems within continue to linger.

The Black community no longer strives for excellence or personal satisfaction; however we cannot stop working to better ourselves, our families, and our community because like it or not, we are playing by white folks rules. Instead of rebelling and ignoring the rules and laws we must follow them because that is the only way we will remain in society. Their plan for us incorporates rebellion, the breaking of laws, and the trail of unsuccessful lives. Murders and convictions make it hard to beat America at her own game; law breaking gives the man the authority to punish our people as they choose. The Black community has to go to school, graduate, attend college, learn a trade, or become an entrepreneur. We need business owners to hire our people-with or without felony convictions; we need people who study our people, people who learn about our children; we need contractors to build the buildings; and we need real estate agents to sell us houses and properties; we need restaurants to serve us lunch; basically we need our education and employment rate to increase. Those people like to make us feel we have no choice and that the cycle of our community is unbreakable. The cycle of chaos is breakable and it shall be proven.

PUBLIC ASSITANCE

CHAPTER 16

History Lesson:

In the 1800s needy families were basically on their own and the government provided assistance in rare cases. Since welfare did not exist there was no unemployment for laid off workers, no food stamps to help them provide food for their families, or no housing assistance to ensure shelter. People had to be self-reliant. Social welfare did not come in to play in to the 1960s when the federal government launched a massive effort to help poor, elderly, and disabled Americans. Social welfare spending increased dramatically between 1970 and 1992 from about 1.5 million to1.3 trillion; tens of millions received some form of assistance through programs such as Medicaid, Medicare, head start, food stamps, school lunches, low-income housing assistance, job training, and Aid families with Dependent children. By the 1980s, many were angry about the large amounts of money spent on Federal anti-poverty programs because federal spending had created a cycle of dependency.

Generations of poor families chose to remain on welfare than become self-sufficient.

Public assistance programs are open to all American citizens in need of it. Many think that the majority of American citizens who receive assistance are Black and a certain stereotype comes to mind when one hears the word welfare: a Black women with a bunch of kids who sits at home and does nothing but wait on a check and food stamps; while on the other hand, whites receive over half of the money the government hands out. Society again points the finger at Blacks to cover the truth that racist use these stereotypes to keep the gap between Black and white living standards. Whites are said to be more worthy in their reasons for needing assistance and are more justifiable while Blacks are undeserving free loaders whose financial state is self-inflicted and should not be eligible for assistance. Outlawed discrimination in hiring preference keep Blacks out of jobs and white collar work fields. America at work.

What people do and say in order to get the assistance or who is receiving the assistance is not my complaint. My annoyance is with the recipients who have no intentions on one day not needing it. To receive the assistance one must be in a certain economic state; therefore one must remain in that state in order to continue receiving the assistance. Welfare has become socially acceptable to Black folks and considered cool (depending on who you ask) to rely on the government (white folks). Is becoming a recipient generation after generation a fashion? Absolutely not!! There are so many who receive benefits from every program and decide to just sit at home and live off the couple dollars they get every month; stay at a dead end job because of not having to work hard; and find comfort and contentment in meritocracy. The Black community is filled with beings who try at nothing other than what they have been doing; deciding to live in low budget housing, complaining about the environment/neighborhood, police and schools yet never putting forth effort to better the financial situation, the children, or ourselves. What a good example we are setting for one another and the children we provide for. Like slavery; white people can put us where ever and we will live there no matter how the bad the conditions and sometimes worsen the conditions. The is always going to be those in need of assistance but the percentage and the length of time it is needed is my concern. The cycle of dependency needs to be broken.

Welfare cripples our community and incriminates our men. On assistance applications there is a space designated for the absent parent. Why?? In order to get any help from Uncle Sam the absent parent has to be placed on child support and in our community the absent parent is mostly our men. Nothing is wrong with child support whether paying or receiving but should be discussed before hand, if possible. For those whose absent parent magically disappeared do what you have to do; on the other hand there are so many in our community who begin or add to criminal records thanks to Uncle Sam and the welfare system. Spitefulness, upset women, peer pressure, miscommunication, misunderstanding, arguments, fights, hear say, etc are the source of so many child support cases. What is best for the children is often looked over. Our women and men need to step us as women, men, and parents and get over the childishness that causes pain, hurt, and confusion in our children by dealing with family issues with maturity.

Receiving public assistance is necessary in cases that have homes with multiple children and a single parent and assistance will continue to be needed because of children out of wedlock and/or divorce; but everyone on welfare has an opportunity to better their financial situation. Casual sex, laziness, and misguidance have young single poor mothers racing to DHS offices around the nation trying to feed and provide for their family because they have robbed themselves of a fair chance due to the obstacles and hurtles that confront parents-men and women—when they have children and are not mentally and most importantly not financially prepared. Parents get overwhelmed with the reality of being a parent and take the easy or less demanding way route in providing for children; while still living the unrealistic reality that they have adopted—which sometimes ends in child neglect-

OUR DEMISE

CHAPTER 17

The Absent Man

I cannot blame all the self-destructive actions of our children(especially boys) on the absent father; but his absence is highly relative in children's behavior and success. Many of our children are lift with an empty space because men leave after their sperm donation. How can so many men know that there is a child (ren) whose DNA make-up matches and they have the slightest idea of who they may be; or know their children but make no attempts to have any type of relationship; or run off and leave their children to be a father to someone else's child; or be a father to some children instead of all. As a community could we raise our children not to make the same mistake? So many Black men grew up without a father but allow their children to live the same unfortunate life. Children with only one active parent figure are left to learn so much on their own. Dads are not there to offer guidance or give advice; and due to the absent man our young men are influenced by the latest

96

popular fashion and hottest celebrity(s). Either its over sized sagging pants revealing underwear covered by a an oversized shirt or its tight sagging pants and shirt that is quite snug. Our young men have no one to teach them how to be a honest noble man; there are no men around to encourage our young boys to stay in school; and our women are busy trying to be mommy and daddy. What our community of boys see are men who are non-graduates and men who work dead end jobs all their life. However a man does not have to make 70k a year to show young boys that there are alternatives to streets and give them an example of what a honest hardworking man looks like. Homes have no dad and the older brother lives life in the streets and is to busy to give the stay in school speech.

All children need guidance and encouragement but what ever a child is exposed to and the life they live will be all that a child knows. Children need to see more than a hood rich life and go farther than the nearest Wal-Mart. Can we at least make sure the children are in school progressing? To many children in the Black community (and the world) are being neglected and abandoned. Parenthood is a hard job no matter if there both parents; but parents are giving up and much of our children's trail and error could be avoided if parents would be there physically, emotionally, and financially. Black men—young and old—take penitentiary chances but do not take children into consideration; worry more about balling, having the latest fashion, liquor, weed, and cigarettes than weather their children have pampers and wipes; are more willing to chance freedom with a life of crime instead of completing high school. In the 21st century our children still do not know how to read a book or write a paragraph but can drop out, sell drugs, and make babies. Those young boys probably are fatherless; don't know or care who their father is; never seen their biological father; or father is dead or in jail. When ANY man of ANY color, of ANY religion, of ANY social class do not spend time and take care of the children they made; they are ABANDONING them. It takes a man to make a child and it takes a man to raise a child.

Drugs

Despite the persona portrayed by television, movies, and music; drugs are killing our community. Being able to afford expensive material things is not worth the damage one may bring upon themselves, family, friends, and community when involving illegal drug activity. Death or jail is most often the end result of drug dealers and users; Life sentences are being handed out like sack lunches everyday in America to drug dealers; and many are under 25. Jeezy enlightened fans that the government will give more time to drug dealers than murderers. Whites reap profit and satisfaction from our community slowly deteriorating. Every one of us dead is one less they have to worry about; every one of us locked up is one more they have seized control over and can profit from because once arrested the future of that person lies in the hands of police report, a judge, and possibly jurors. Lawbreakers, mentally ill correction facilities, and prisoners are gold mines for white people. Dealers could at least stick together in their activities instead of beefing. At least then the survival chances would increase.

Once locked up all the so-called "friends" disappear. Little to none of them write, visit, let alone send money. If released those same "friends" show up at the welcome home party eating, drinking, and talking about what they would have done if it were them. Paying for collect calls, making visiting appointments, working to put money on books, daily worrying, and explaining to everyone how and why things happened are the burdens dealers leave on the ones who love them. Addicts bring pain and suffering. Everyday addicts give birth to babies who are born on drugs. Those children one day become emotionally and some physically scared for life because of parents' addiction. Addicts become thieves, prostitutes, liars, deceivers, and treacherous to any and every one. Offered help goes unwanted and their families are left watching addicts loose their mind to drugs.

Dealers and addicts are like cancer and our community is the body. They are slowly but surely killing us.

Drugs in our community is another form of social control. 1st the government makes our children feel there is no way out; Mothers are struggling, fathers are no where to be found, and children have to help make sure the bill gets paid. 2nd they suck our young adolescents in the to drug dealing for quick easy money. Dealing becomes cool and full of glamour because of all the stuff that money can buy, so it attracts more candidates. (The more people who commit crimes of illegal drug activity are the more people who can be arrested, hell many of our young men do not push enough weight to call themselves drug dealers, but enjoy the title and attention from peers.) 3rd our community gets hooked on the drugs and become addicts. Though they are addicts, they are still mothers, fathers, aunts, uncles, cousins, etc. If the parents are on drugs who is left to raise the children? 4th the government arrests our men and women seeking maximum punishments and jail time. With so many of our people behind bars it leaves our community broken, torn, and forgotten.

* Some Black men become dealers, in police eyes; because of color, the model car, and the side of town.

The government will not legalize drugs due to the profit margin. Stores will never price match cocaine, or show weed prices in local sales papers. My advice: 1. STOP SNITCHING. Dealers need to have a nationwide communication and understanding and work through situations without violence. Conflict resolution. If no one is talking and letting local police in on drug activity then investigations are harder to close. Situations will arise and people will get caught up but dealers need to be cautious and work together.

2. STOP SELLING DRUGS. The chances of this happening are slim to none, but we are really tearing down our community when we feed addicts addiction. We must love and help one another. If everyone stopped then addicts would be forced to quit or go elsewhere. Maybe a long shot but it is possible. It would become one less crime white people could trail us for. Also, ALL of our people are capable of so much more than handling drugs and drug abuse. Every one of us is destined to be great.

Murder

The murder rate in the Black community is outrageous; the kills are Black on Black and people are dying for ridiculous indifferences. Some murderers seem to think they are the Almighty and have the knowledge and discretion to decide when it is time for another's man soul to leave to earth. The reasons for these murders are the most heartbreaking; people are dying over $5. As pitiful as it may sound; with out considering the amount, people are killing and dying over sheets of paper that do not descend with the soul upon death. Killing has become popular, especially in the hip-hop culture. Murdering has become acceptable among peers and many are shooting for popularity, respect, and favor. The motives behind murder are not ever reasonable nor does it change the fact that one becomes a murderer and that crime is punishable by law; although, some are killing because they have to practice what they preach in the presence of friends watching, not wanting to risk looking lame or weak in their eyes. Disagreements and fights happen and a lot of B.S. could be avoided if someone would walk away; shooting and stabbing is overboard often never being worth the consequences that follow. Rapper T.I. is a perfect example.

At some point or another we have to grow up and realize a person does not deserve to be shot because they upset you or won a fight. Everybody takes a lose at one time or another and shooting will not change the emotions felt or fact that they won and you lost. Conflict resolution. Our cities and its inhabitants; young and old, are going to hell everyday in the Black community who live in and by the world; live in and by the streets; then kill one another's unsaved souls.

Movies, television, and music—mostly gansta rap—are once again negatively influencing the Black community (and the world). The C.D. does not come with a 22 but it may as well. Rappers are pretending to be ganstas, hood niggas, and thugs in their music and in videos by False fully describing the consequences of any and everyone who "dis" respects them; and in doing so, they have created problems in our community. Listeners are running around trying to live out the lyrics of songs; not thinking about their actions or the consequences that follow, and it is beyond stupid. We will all die one day; it will at different times, in different ways and for different reasons, but can stupid shit stop being the reason people (young and old; black and white) are losing their life. Peers and gansta rap encourage one another to commit crimes and murders for retaliation, drugs, money, jealousy, deceit, and ultimately immaturity but quick trills equal life sentences. On top of it all; everything is all fun and games until someone we know is hurt or killed. When it is someone we know then everybody want to act a fool and the violated or killed victims did not deserve it. NEWS FLASH: NOBODY DESERVES TO DIE AT THE HAND OF ANOTHER MAN! Our ancestors did not survive slavery, Jim Crow, and separate but equal for us to die at the hand of each other.

Jail

Last but not least; imprisonment contributes to the failing and decreasing size of the Black community. Jail destroys the family structure and explains where the absent parent is. People are in jail for one or two reasons: 1. innocent or 2. guilty. Guilty parties: Why commit the crime in the first place? Sometimes unfortunate events eventually lead to committing a crime but we have a choice even though America's society has a way of making us feel like we do not. All crimes are punishable by law and no one ever intends to get caught but that is always a possibility. Why risk the little freedom and ties to the outside world for a petty crimes that are not worth the legal procedures of courts or the time in jail. Politicians are passing bills and laws focusing on making less serious crimes punishments more severe. The crimes that are priority are crimes being committed in low-income neighborhoods vs. middle and upper class neighborhoods.

Prisons are not owned by the government but by private owned companies; prisons are a multi-billion dollar industry and tax payers pay for prisons. Company owners have political ties are lobbyist; steaming the political corruption. Mental ill patients are used as lab rats for medical experimentation for pharmaceutical drugs and inmates have to do what they are told because the prison has control over them. Prison owners and the consumer market live for people to go to jail because prisoners are free/cheap labor with no labor laws. Correctional facilities provide work for little pay doing jobs that are profitable to many different consumer markets. And the Black community act like it is a right of passage to have a criminal record and/or do time in jail. Why would anyone want to be under the control of another man? Prisoners have little to no rights and incarceration is legal enslavement. Officers and guard can harass and mistreat who ever they choose for what ever reason they choose. The food, clothing, and housing facilities provide meet the minimum criteria and inmates live like animals in a zoo divided into cages(ceils/pods).

Jail appreciates the dollar value. Collect calls are over priced, fines are outrageous amounts, and bonding out (with the ten percent) calls for to much damn money. Rappers like Lil Wayne; who made 20million, are the only ones who make money in prison; the average person loses. Rap music has incarcerated many who glorify and admire the music with actions. Our community thinks it is an achievement by living the outlandish lyrics; the music promotes the nonchalant attitudes toward one another and law enforcement; and our community glamorizes life behind bars and the chaos that comes with it. WAKE UP!

Prisons place most Black men in the hole and there is 23 hour lock down for prisoners to think for the rest of the prison sentence; 4 out of 10 young Black men are caught in the justice system and that is 8xs the rate of whites; police line us up and lock us up to be put in front of an appointed judge to decide the fate of our future; final breathes are taken behind prison bars; our ex-cons get out with very slim odds of finding a job and are sometimes forced back into the life of crime just to survive; Parole and probations still have ex-cons under supervision and on a short leech. America will do what ever it takes to grasp us in her twisted justice system. Bottom line: there are more Blacks in jail than in college. Blacks committing crimes and becoming habitual offenders in society has us throwing our lives away. Our community has juveniles serving life sentences. SAD!! Most prisoners never had a chance at life; are never able to reach their true potential; are ruining generations to come because the people that needed them were in the free world while they are left inside the prison walls.

Men are very important factors in the family structure and without there presence families, our community, and the world is affected by that absence. Black men are still powerful beings that bring a different flavor and meaning to any and all things that they involve themselves with especially if it is positive and is pursued by a good hard working Black man. Our community needs leadership and guidance but our community also needs to build up Black men and not write them off the way society and the world has. Positive words and positive role models are what the males of color need; not role models of men who want to be idolized and worshipped. Men of color with influence have to become a guiding light and an example though example;

not by showing off with money, materials, weapon, power, and fear with a gansta swag. Our community of boys and men have to display love, care, and look out for one another instead of setting one another up. Black men have to accept one another especially if they are in a state of poverty instead if bullying and putting one another down. Older males have to look out and help out younger males by telling them what is right and encouraging them to complete school and tell them to do their best. The men have to take care of the boys because the women can only do so much. We are all hurting but through love we can be healed.

SEE NO EVIL

CHAPTER 18

It appears that maturity and age are no longer determining factors in what is viewed by our children. Daily television shows have evolved and now very little is considered inappropriate. Intimacy on television is nearly porn, women are damn near exposed, scripts are written with no language barriers; basically one can say or do just about anything. Artificial dramas dominate majority of the cable channels; crime investigation dramas paint misleading images of police and courtroom procedures; scenes are illusive yet fact-full in revealing methods of different law enforcement, their investigations and tactics, viewers still do not know their Rights. Networks may argue that it is a new day and age, yeah it is a new day but our children are having children, fighting, killing, dropping out, cursing, running away, and throwing away their future at younger and younger ages. Everything looks and sounds 100x better on screens than reality, but those words and images are implanted in young viewers' brain who leave home hoping to live lives as those they have seen on television. The entertainment industry is not taking responsibility and/ or not realizing the impact television has on America as a whole.

Fictitious dramas, movies, and reality television has taken over the cable channels. The Black community entertainers are displayed variously but not very few roles betray a truthful light of Blacks and the way we live today. Predominantly white cast shows portray Blacks to be white-collar upper middle class; predominantly Black cast shows portray blue-collar jobs that are either middle class or lower middle class; segregated shows cast one Black in a sea of whites; or the show is all white or all Black. Very few shows actually show the way the average Black family lives and television broadcasts either are above or below average with Black life. Where are the daily ordeals that do not end in a drive by shootings? Network writers and producers should begin to diversify television and movies, and actually resemble the way Black people really live.

Disregarding what is broadcasted; parents need to stop using television as a babysitter for children. Many parents are unaware of what their children are watching, but wonder where all of these bad habits and unexplained behavior is originating. Television is teaching our children to kiss, give them dating advice, give them revenge methods, help to create ideas involving illegal activity, and help with social boundaries in school. As parents we have a lot of responsibilities but we cannot get so consumed and wrapped up in our own lives that we forget our children need us more than an electric box.

Weapon

"Believe half of what you see and none of what you hear" is a quote not exercised by America or her citizens. America believes what she wants especially if it is in favor of her way of thinking. The documentaries and journalist entries are not promoted in the news and the truth goes unrecognized. The government and Satan use the media as a brainwashing tool to keep people in fear, lost, undecided, and in the dark; with altered truths with holding the information keeping Americans in a stereotypical mind frame; and media televise stories in different lights according to color. Whites are most often portrayed as helpless victims when guilty or wrong. Blacks are portrayed as thugs and ganstas even if innocent. The media is utilized as a cover up tool in America's corrupted government; documents, pictures, videos, and reports are ceased and the American people are distracted with bogus fabricated stores. The truth is covered up and lies are told until they become believable. The media is one of the most dangerous weapons in our country and is one of the most efficient. We have all believed some of the stories broadcasted and take the advice of the news in how we can protect ourselves from the boosted awareness of people and things in the reports. Subliminal messaging is a weapon of Satan. Fashion and media hide underline truths and deceptions of Satan. The devil's deceit has Americans living in his image, watching his image, and wearing his image. People are unaware that they are being misguided and can not repent and be forgiven for living of this world.

HIP-HOP IN AMERICA

CHAPTER 19

Hip-Hop is one of the most influential genres of music in the world and one of the few things Black people can call their own. In spite of populartity; Hip-hop is dying due to the depreciating value. Hip-hop has lost authentic-ness; needing a form of reincarnation FAST! Hip-Hop has sold its soul and artist are cloned copy cats. Uniqueness, creativity, and originality are primary ingredients to Hip-Hop, but now everyone looks and sounds the same. Vocalist and songwriters give little to no thought to lyrics, not to mention the videos. Different races and ethnic groups listen and make Hip-Hop, but our community is stereotyped by the music and videos. Rappers characterize themselves as thugs in the music and dress in thug gear; then anyone who dresses in their image is automatically labeled as a thug. Of course; people should be more open-minded instead of ignorant, and know that all Black people are not fans of Hip-Hop and those people who are, are not all thugs. America's ignorance; however has taken a negative toll on our community.

Same 'ol Story

Gansta rap artist should be more universal instead of everyone talking about the EXACT same thing. Money, women, violence, and drugs occupy about 90% of rappers lyrics. When one looks past the cursing, some songs have actual meaning; but that is not the case for majority of rappers. A Large percentage of the lyrics talk about the same garbage on every single song leaving the album worthless. The crazy thing is; many listeners actually believe the lyrics. Rappers have become compulsive competitive LAIRS. Most of what is seen and none of what is heard have little to any truth; and rappers ridiculously redundantly holla how real and how true they are. Okay, if artist are so real then why are such a large percent of your rhymes a lie?? These artists claim to sell drugs and don't know cocaine from baby powder; do not know how to boil water let alone cook crack—but many are quick to talk about how much weight they moving; some rappers are scared of the dark but claim they fight and shoot people; rappers boost about their money but rap about robbing and stealing. Come on. Guess it is just a competition of who can put on the biggest front. Can fans please hear the truth instead of a bunch of words that rhyme on a beat? There are artist with criminal records and do or have committed crimes talked about in their music; nonetheless bragging about a criminal record is foolish. Can we brag about a diploma, A.C.T. scores or a degree? When did not meeting the minimum requirements to become a high school graduate become cool? In the real world a criminal record keeps our community from attaining a far chance in the work-field. Rappers lyrics are lies and some listeners either live that life or are pretending to live that life but rappers do not have to worry about job applications. The music needs to mature.

Aspiring Rappers

RAPPING IS NOT FOR EVERYONE!!! A toddler can rhyme, but rap is a creative form of self-expression. People really sound like B-Rad off the movie "Malibu's Most Wanted" and think they will go platinum or get a record deal. Just because peers like it does not mean it should be recorded and distributed. A lot of rappers dropped out of school, turned to the streets, and made it to rap: PLEASE BE AWARE: This does not work for everyone; STAY IN SCHOOL! If one cannot read a menu how can one read a million dollar contract? Aspiring onlookers who just want the money FYI: the people we do not see really make the money. At some point we have to want more than what is seen on TV and what is heard on the radio. Hip-Hop will surely die if every new artist is trying to be like the last. Hip-Hop is suffering in more ways than one, it does not need a wanna be gansta, a mannish rapper who can only talk about sex, a person pretending to live a lavish fairytale life, or a person whose vocabulary is that of a elementary student and only refer to women in disrespectful terms. Hip-Hop is capable of so much more. Dare to be different. Hip-Hop needs real artists who are serious about the music.

Beef

Beef comes from a cow. LOL. Seriously Beef is an unnecessary negative element of Hip-Hop. When rappers

Beef it stirs up a lot of confusion in our community. Listeners begin to pick sides and feel they have to defend their favorite artist (due to the fact that the favorite rapper is unlikely to be present.) and conversations about the Beef escalate and violence has been the end result in some case; even though rappers could give a rat's ass bout listeners. The origin is most Beefs are asinine but with the help of the media it is transformed into a world war. Hip-Hop artist fear their image or being looked at as weak or pussy and entertain the nonsense; parties that start the Beef are seeking attentions and have nothing better to do with their time. Answer me this: If rappers have all this money, all these women, and are selling all these drugs when is their time to make dis-records about another artist? Successful grown men and women arguing through lyrics and beats achieves what? And there is enough negativity in the Black community. Participating in Beef is petty and immature no matter who started it and America has seen Beefs taken too far and innocent people got physically hurt or threatened. Artists have become horrible examples for fans and promote stereotypes America has branded on the Black community. Beef has no place in Hip-Hop.

Bitches and Hoes

A bitch is a female dog. Women are guilty of being only one thing in that definition, a female. With that being said, why are rappers always talking about their female dogs in their song? Male artists are:

- Having sex with them—illegal and sick.

- Beating them—animal brutality and animal cruelty. Illegal.
- Breeding them for money—that is pimping. Illegal
- Taking one another's female dogs—that is stealing. Illegal
- Taking them to Petco getting their fur and nail done-this is just weird.

Since when did these four legged creature move up on the food chain? Regardless of whom rappers are referring to in their lyrics, it is frequently assumed they are talking about Black women. The acts of women described in songs are acts that all women commit, but since Hip-Hop is Black music, Blacks are stereotyped. For rappers that are talking about Black women, hear me and hear me well: WE ARE NOT BITCHES. That word is loosely thrown around daily in conversations, arguments, and music; however, Hip-Hop is the only music genre that degrades their women in such a manner. What did Black women do to not get addressed by name. If it is not a female dog it is another animal; chicken head, hood rat, duck, pigeon etc. On the surface the word is socially acceptable but under the surface the use of these words in music is teaching young boys that women are bitches and tells young girls that it is ok to be called names. Even when rappers are congratulating or praising women, her title still ends in bitch: Gutta Bitch, Gansta Bitch, 5 Star Bitch, Down Bitch etc. Is this the only word that comes to our men minds when describing a woman? Should women stop naming their daughter because they are only going to be called bitches in the future? Maybe bitch should be printed on the birth certificate. Artists and our men need to give us the respect we deserve. Whenever our men ready to eat, need clean clothes, need sex, or just someone to talk to they turn to the very same women they degrade and disrespect. Our Black women have been standing beside our Black men when they are jobless, homeless, car less, broke, uneducated, fatherless, and emotionally broken since slavery and our men say thank you by calling our women female dogs. It is one thing to use bitch, but our men scream it over beats and the usage of the word has gotten outrageous.

Hoes are a different story. Let us be honest, there are hoes and some rappers are referring to actual women when rapping about certain endeavors. Some of our women are gold digging hoes, freak hoes, nasty hoes etc. nonetheless it is not only Black women who fit that category. Once again, America makes assumptions by what is heard from our urban artist. It is unbalanced because America assumes our women are loose but in the girl gone wild commercials white girls reveal themselves while getting drunk. Oh I forgot there is a double standard when it comes to their women. As for rappers who are quick to label women for their sex acts; artist are in the same boat. Bragging about nasty women and the sex makes men just as nasty and the rhyming lyrics are shameful on men and women. Men have become just a big a hoe as women. It is disrespectful to rap about their women in that negative light because nobody has to know what women are doing behind closed doors, regardless of race. Stop rapping for record sells and popularity; ignoring the bad effects that the music world has on our community.

Profit

White people are really reaping the profit off of Hip-Hop. Those people are not concerned with the state of our community nor do they care how the music is putting our community's future at risk. RECORD SALES are up! Sex sells so record companies do not care how many teenage mothers were influenced by records. RECORD SALES are up! Gun and drug talk sells but CEOs do not care how many of our young men die or are locked away because of violent music. RECORD SALES are up! Those people are not concerned with how our women are degraded and disrespected. RECORD SALES are up! As long as record sells are up, all of us could burn in hell. Harsh but true. White people are doing what they have always done. Make money off of us and live well while we suffer.

In Da Hood

It is silly how rappers are always talking about being in the hood and lying about it. Rappers act like being in the hood and living the "hood rich" is cool and it is not. Please stop rapping that hood life is the "way to live" mainly because rappers do not live like that. Rappers do not want to be criticized for not being in the hood, but why lie about it in the first place. People who actually reside in the hood wish everyday they did not have to listen to gun shots, see violence on the streets daily, watch the police harass and arrest peers, have drug dealers control streets and corners, watch crack heads wonder the streets day in and day out, and see people jailed. Rappers have money; yet pretend to be in the hood, and shoot videos in projects that they know nothing about. Rappers that are in the hood certainly do not live there; however hood niggas eat up the music and never attempt to leave the hood or get out of the streets. Brand new system, rims, TV's and cars with fresh paint jobs but living in a HUD house is absurd. Hood rich is an irresponsible way to live but rap lyrics glamour and promote the lifestyle. People spend money to appear a certain way to peers and resemble entertainers, videos, and magazines but this irresponsible living has our community suffering drastically and illegal activity is how many are willing to pay for this lifestyle. People are stealing to sell, buying stolen goods, and doing what ever it takes to afford the glamour and glitz seen and heard by artists. Rappers and their listeners have diluted their life, purpose, and thought process.

Sex

Sex is another factor that is destroying our community. Sex is idolized and considered to be a way to fit in for adolescents to call themselves men and women. Books from authors like Zane; who has an amazing way with words, turn sex into a mental daydream and makes one feel as if they are on a weightless never ending cloud of paradise. These books have reached the hands of teenage girls leaving them suspicious and provoking premature sexual awakenings. Rappers making comments like "what this girl won't do another will," making young girls feel like they should be lucky to receive attention of guys; teasing girls for deciding to wait on sex; is sending girls on a road of trail and error. R&B artist are just as guilty. Step by steps lyrics on what to do and how to do it fill radio countdowns. Sex sells but at what cost? Our youth are paying the ultimate price because the music encourages casual sex and numerous partners. Early unprotected sex activity leads to diseases and children having children. Videos of half naked pretty girls prancing around makes girl feel that looking like what they have seen is the only way to feel sexy or good about themselves. Female entertainers are guilty as well. Over exposure of the body and lyrics that are sometime more explicit than male encourages young female listeners to engage in sexual acts believing it is ok. Where is the positive music to encourage our young girls and boys that sex can be dangerous and that there is no rush because they are worth waiting for.

White Rappers

Hip-Hop has influenced nearly every race and cultures all around the world have their own version of Hip-Hop. Once again Hip-Hop is not for everyone. It is offensive when I hear whack white rappers pretending to lead a life never lead. It is a mockery of our music and our community when rappers characterize themselves as ganstas because they have on large clothing, cars with rims, claiming to be hood, and what ever other nonsense. I rarely find it funny when I hear white rappers being whack purposely. The "White Rapper Show" on VH1 showed America that most white people cannot rap. Just listen to the music if you are not truly talented. There are enough whack Black rappers, whack white rappers just make it worst.

Famous Not Rich

Record labels are advising rappers to sign contracts only to deceive them. Labels take advantage of up coming artist because labels know artists are ignorant to the rules, procedures, and tactics of the industry; which leave artist high and dry. Some artists who are stuck in contracts are similar to sharecroppers. Legal advisors are put in place to gain trust and help artist sign bogus contracts; Labels purposely make verbal promises telling artist everything they want to hear but it is not written in the contract; Executives also put deadlines on the contracts putting artist under pressure rushing them into an impulsive decision; Labels sit back and reap all the profits while the artists do the legwork; Labels also invest more time in money in certain artist more than others and it is not based on talent; Budgets are really loans from record companies and so are the advances; Advances are how some artists are broke—After giving an advance, companies are also making artist foot their own bill for nearly EVERYTHING leaving them in debt and once record sales begin to take off so does the cut for the executives. They tell you how much money you are going to get but failing to mention the expenses. If an artist does not meet or exceed the loan then there may not be a second album anytime soon. Many label executives do not even listen to the music outside of work and some may not listen at all. Labels look at what and who is popular and run with it; which means they are only looking at numbers. Many signed artists do not have the type of financial support, guidance, or equipment for people to even hear their music nationally or globally; because under contract their music is basically handicapped. Some signed artists are unable to make independent music leaving them unheard. Since contracts are almost impossible to get out of, artists are unable to produce new music thus eliminating the competition. The Trick: Labels never intend for certain artist to succeed. Companies are signing artist to gain control of their music and the labels "favorite" artist—who is dominating the charts and bringing in all the money for the label—will remain the favorite. Independent artist and labels with a new sound, new people, and a new trend are the competition but if all who are independent are signed then the major companies seize control of the music. That leaves the popular, popular and the new unheard of.

Hip-Hop and R&B artist of the Black community fall for this trickery everyday. Our upcoming artists are so busy looking at money, cars, clothes, and fame of other artists; they forget to read the FINE print. Anxiousness has artist making quick unthough-out decisions. Those people are once again using poverty and the "American Dream" to rob us of much more than our money. Those people use the influence of famous people in our community to prematurely expose our children to a fantasy life of sex, money, drugs, and flashy materials. Our community has to come to the reality of what is really taken place and how it is affecting our children and our community as a whole

What Happened

Black music has become corrupt. One reason America is afraid of Blacks is because our music tells the world that our men are thieves, who carry guns, and will kill anyone no matter how simple or complex the problem maybe; All our guys do is smoke weed and/or sell drugs; All our women have no morals or values and will do anything as long as the man has money or at least look like he does. Our female rappers basically agree when they boast and brag about the exact same crap as our men. Though most of the lyrics are fables, America sees it as reality merely by the way some of us dress. Recognizing that America encourages failure upon us; our music just gives fuel to that ridiculous stereotypical fire.

Hip-Hop was supposed be a form of self-expression. A person could say how they felt about anything from politics to roaches. Now it has become a competition and game over money. Artist are always talking about materials, what they would do, or have done but hardly anyone talks about how they feel. Gansta rap is full of threats and violence like artist want fights to break out in the club. The music is encouraging blatant disrespect while also telling listeners if some one disrespects them some act of violence should be committed against them. Hip-Hop is no longer that fun different sound one could just sit back and listen to. Skill is no longer a requirement. The music industry is only concerned with the money.

Hip-Hop and the 10 Commandments

The Ten Commandments were instructions from God directing the people on how to live and if they live by those commandments man would be able to live among one another in peace. The Ten Commandments are still the instructions from God for man and if all men lived by those principles the world would be a better place. It is obvious that man—believers or non believers—have ignored these instructions and would rather live the way they choose despite the havoc it causes generation after generation.

Hip-hop music has become an influence thoughout the world with a strong impact on the minds, the decisions, and the actions of even those who are not listeners of the genre. So many words of Hip-hop have become negative and speak profaneness over what is right in the eyes of the Lord.

The Ten Commandments:

1. ***Thou shall have no other Gods before me.***
   Hop-hop often thrives off negativity, rebellion, and material worldly gain. Idolizing materials, money, women, drugs, and one another based on the views and opinions of society and peers and show no respect or regard to God, who He is, or what He said do. Hip-hop worships and idolizes itself and selfish lifestyles—the music and party scene, the money, and other worldly things that money can buy.

2. ***Thou shall not make for yourself a carved image—any likeness of anything that is in heaven above, or that is in the earth beneath, or the water under the earth.*** 2 words—Jesus piece. The world has done its best to depict what Jesus could have looked liked but has gotten it wrong because the world does not know what Jesus looked liked *damn sure not in the last 16 centuries. Hip-Hop has placed the worlds picture of Jesus in to chunks of metal filled with diamonds; while still promoting violence, murder, fortification, and rebellion. Charms of Jesus are overblown, ignorant due to lack of knowledge, and disrespectful due to unrighteousness and social prejudices. Rosary beads

have become fashionable and clothing is plastered with ungodly and subliminal images. God does not receive worship for His creations but the world worships one another and materials and Hip-Hop seats the stage.

3. ***Do not take the name of the Lord your God in vain.*** Hip-hop (and movies) does not only use the name of God in vain, but also speak out against His name, His power, and His creations. To swear upon anything. Matthew 5:34-37 *But I say unto you, swear not at all; neither by heaven; for it is God's throne; (35) Nor by the earth; for it is His footstool; Neither by Jerusalem; for it is the city of the great King. (36)Neither shall you swear by thy head, because you can not make it white nor black (37) But let your communication be Yes, yes, No, no; for whosoever is more than these cometh of evil.* People-period—loosely use the name of God in meaningless worthless conversations, debates, arguments, fights, and lyrics that have nothing to do with God, who He is, and what He stands for. This commandment is about respect for God, His authority, and respect for the relationship man has for God. Hip-hop is full of disrespect toward God, toward another man and/or women, and toward the artist themselves. The Father, The Son, and The Holy Spirit bring power and presence when man calls upon their name; lyrics with crime, violence, murder, disrespect, threats, sex, money, drugs, nonsense, boosting and bragging, and/or deceit need not to call on the presence and power of the three.

4. ***Remember the Sabbath day and keep it Holy.***
Jesus clarified that it is o.k. to work if necessary on the Sabbath, notwithstanding the debate of which day exactly does the Sabbath fall on—Saturday or Sunday? Hip-hop has promoted the illusion that everyday is a day to party, drink, drug, and commit acts of fornication. Hip-hop has also made it more cool to make it rain at the club—which basically and literally throws ones money away—than pay tides. Self presentation and possessions and their worth also out measure the amount of money giving in the offering and the helping of other people. I, Me, I, ME, fill the lyrics of songs as if artist are waking themselves up everyday. This commandment is about not becoming selfish and 1. Remember our Creator 2. Acknowledge Him by setting aside one day 3. Keep it Holy by paying respects to our Creator though praise, worship, prayers, and the building of a stronger relationship.

5. ***Honor though mother and father***
Hip-hop's rebellion prevents the ability to honor anyone aside from itself and its material possession—no matter how they were obtained. Hip-Hop lyrics relay advice and suggested behavior; that influence leave the youth out of control. "I don't give a f*#@" and "I do what I want to do" widens the misleading path for all participants of hip-hop. Honor in that verse do not mean just obey them, but it also means to respect and love them. Deception and Dishonor="What they do not know wont hurt 'em." The bible gives consequences for the dishonor but artist and listeners ignore the

commandment, disobey parents and God, all in the name of hip-hop. This commandment teaches respect for parents and other individuals, teaches listening and obeying; helps in guidance of the youth; but hip-hop teaches rebellion. Rebellion= Misguidance=Chaos.

6. ***Thou shall not murder.***
    Gangsta rap lyrics are notorious advocates for murder. Every sentence of every verse and chorus encourage the murder of another man or his loved ones. Hip-hop actually made it popular and fashionable not only to murder but also to brag about taking the life out of the body(s). Gangsta rap boost the act of murder in the dumbest cases; ignorantly hip-hop perceives the violence and deaths from the music as an accomplishment, but to encourage murder is to speak out against God.

7. ***Thou shall not commit adultery.***
    Hip-hop promotes casual sex and discourages marriage. Hip-hop also encourages cheating in committed relationships and in marriages. The music speaks out against marriage and the feelings of being tied down and or the feelings of love; saying "show no love" and love no women. The men and women of hip-hop cheat with groupies who may also be cheating on a spouse; married artist brag about sexual endeavors with other women in their lyrics and portray the single life in videos; and single artist brag about sexual acts with married women as if it is ok. Faithfulness is washed away with "blaming it on the alcohol"; infidelity reigns;

and more children are born into broken homes in the "hood."

8. ***Thou shall not steal.***
Hip-hop is an advocate for this sin also. To steal and rob adds the gangsta status of the artist and the music. Hip-hop motivates listeners who commit crimes; artist pretend to feel the pain/hard times and tell them it is ok to rob. The music gives step by step instructions and glamorized stories of "living a life of crime" and "being in the streets." This again speaks out against God blatantly over beats.

9. ***You shall not bear false witness against your neighbor.***
Neighbor is used in the content and context of ANY persons whether it is friend or foe. Hip-hop and the world see lying as a means of saving ones own ass. Most of the lyrics of hip-hop are a lie and the characters in the lyrics are made up as well. Hip-hop has been set up around fantasy. Artists are not only lying in lyrics but artist and listeners begin to lie to themselves when they desire and attempt to live a life that is based around superficial people and truths.

10. ***You shall not covet your neighbor's house; you shall not covet your neighbor's wife, or his male servant, or his female servant, or his ox, his donkey, or anything that is your neighbor.***
Today's hip-hop is so centered on "look at what I got" and Ha, "look at what you don't have" which embrace disobeying this commandment.

Many more sins unfold from disobeying this commandment such as lust, greed, envy, theft, anger, jealous, and murder. This commandment tells believers to be content and happy with our life and our possessions no matter what our neighbor has. Hip-hop tells us that the desires of the heart should be fulfilled regardless of how "wrong" it may be. "BIGGER IS BETTER" is an underline message in most hip-hop music and relies the illusion that what ever a person has is not enough unless it is the biggest, latest, and/or most expensive leaving all who agree unsatisfied. The breath of life should be satisfaction enough.

Hip-hop music has become unacceptable in the eyes of Lord and is misleading His people. Personal gain and popularity is what hip-hop is now based around. Hip-hop artist have become idols and role models yet speak no truth into our community.

OVER-DUE ALTERATIONS

CHAPTER 20

Change in our community has been the talk for years on end. My question is: How long are we going to talk about it? When is some type of action going to take place?

Everyone in America wants to "move up" and live the "American Dream: Nice house in nice neighborhood, nice car to drive to good job, and nice children that attend nice schools." All that is fine and dandy but of course the American Dream is those peoples dream. I do not feel we have to work to obtain the things that whites have or live where they live if we just take care of what we already have and live were we already live. Lets face it, some of us may never afford to live in certain areas, some are not even physically capable to move, some may always need housing assistance, and some have been in areas all their lives and that is where they call home so can we PLEASE begin to take care of our communities. As we can all see, if we do not care no one will. Our siblings, grandparents, parents, children, and friends have to live, walk, and ride those streets. We can help the way they look so why not make them look nice. How many people take actual pride in our neighborhoods? I am so tired of the never ending griping and complaining about the trash and garbage on the streets yet no one ever volunteers to pick any of it up. When will be able to take pride in saying we live in the projects/hood/ghetto? It is the hood/ ghetto/projects because we made it and allows it to be that way. We destroy and deface the buildings, schools, and houses; Residents throw garbage in vacant lots; our community does not care about lawns; and as far as the maintenance of streets that are to be held up by the cities goes—we have to stop complaining to one another and complain to the city officials. Protest, write letters, sign petitions, what ever it takes to get it done. Those are our children outside on those streets no one else's. There are millions of ways that we can improve our community that may call for a little time, commitment and teamwork.

Schools

Low budgets, shortage of teachers, outdated textbooks, and nonchalant attitudes are all negative characteristics effecting our children's education. Our educators are giving up on our children by doing whatever makes the job easier; instead of correcting their wrongs, schools are allowing children to act in any manner they please. Giving up on the children and their education increases the chance of failure and misguides them into thinking they make the rules no matter where they are. Education employees take pride in your job and do your very best in sending students on the right path PLEASE. Loving those children unconditionally is the key. None of us are perfect especially not children learning the game of life. Students are going to mess up, make the same mistakes over, lash out, lie, give in to peer pressure, and the list goes on but schools have to continue to encourage. Every time a school turns their back on a student they assist sending that child down a road of destruction. "If a man knows nothing, he can be nothing." Illiteracy was and is a double bladed sword to our community and we still have that stain in history when it was against the law for us to learn. Slaves lost their lives for knowing anything other than how to be a slave. A person would have to search hard, far, and long to find a nigger who knew anything worth knowing. History can not repeat it's self. It is time to do better.

For the children who want to drop out and justify it by saying school is not for everyone; I have this to say. You are absolutely right school is not for everyone but knowledge is. Students who think they know everything please stop and take the time to listen. You may learn a thing or two that may help you in the long run. Hell; Most of the stuff you know is not even worth knowing. Please respect and obey those who are trying to be a positive guide to you. Not doing the required work, ignoring the details, and not showing up to school only hurts the person doing it.

Accepting unacceptable behavior is the source of many problems and keeps our children behind. Cannot forget about the unconcerned parents. Complaining about what the teacher is not doing, yet never taking the time to look at what the parent could do the help the children should be frowned upon. We can set up tutorials in our homes. We need to take out the time to find out what out children really need instead of looking at the school to make sure our children succeed. A teacher's job is to teach the criteria set by the state while equipping the child with whatever else they may need in the world but success is the job of the parent.

We have to stop giving up on our children; seeing that they are our future. There will be no future if our children do not straighten up.

Attitudes

Blacks are just as racist as whites. As a community we have to change our outlook on each other and the world. It has proven itself hard to build up one another when you have been torn down all your life but we must offer one another support instead of gossip talk. The attitude of our community and its condition is not a proactive one and we have turned on each other. Some of us have lost sight of the important things; our lack of concern and not seeking answers is part of the main problem. We are living for the next day and not for the future that we will not be apart of because we are to busy worrying about the wrong things. There is no superman to swoop in and make everything better we have to better ourselves and the community will become better itself.

Grown Folks

24/8 and 365 a year Black children are delivered in the midst of childish drama between adults. Lies, cheaters, verbal and physical abuse, senseless conflict, family feuds, who is the daddy controversy, physical straps, and immature acts are unfit environments surrounding innocent children, and "grown folks" are only concerned with proving points and getting revenge on one another. The children are the ones who are getting hurt. Witnessing reasonless drama sorrowfully leaves serious emotional scars on our children; which places a negative effect on our community. Today our men are not in the lives of children; reasons may vary, but some mothers are not permitting the child to be with the father behind spiteful reasons. Some women feel that if the father is not their finically then he cannot be there at all. That is absolutely absurd. Only factual solid reason should a child not spend time with their father. A child has needs that need to be met financially, but that is not the child's fault or responsibility. Children need the love and attention from both parents and material things are not always that important when compared to children essential relationship with parents. The court system does not always have to solve our problems; especially when it involves our children. Parents will never always do everything right and childish antics ruin bridges between separated parents. Parents are held up and holding on to past situations and past issues; unmasking and exposing dirty laundry to any and everyone who will listen. "Grown folks" are constantly reminding one another of past mistakes and spitefully enlighten children to create troubled thoughts in children. What ever the problems are between parents should stay among parents. It is not fair for the child to be drug into the middle of childish drama, so get over or work out the drama for the sake of our children who may one day become parents. Bad mouthing the other parent to or in front of the child is the BIGGEST mistake a parent can make. Regardless of what the parent does or has done is crap children do not need to hear. These children did not ask to be here or to be used as ponds by childish parents. Parents should not be sending messages through children putting them in the middle of their mess. Parents have become divided and are even unable to be in one another's presence. As a parent one could probably write a book about everything the other parent does wrong; however at the end of the day, all 365 a year, both of you are the parent and must do what is best for the child (ren) not what makes you feel better. Once the female conceives both participating parties are bound together forever. People are upset and eventually dislike the other parent, and it is ones own fault. Should have given more thought into who one lay down with.People are not looking at the type of parent their partner may be and look only at what is amusing at that time. My momma told me: The same person you having sex with is not the same person you have a baby by and the same goes for marriage and divorce.

Many mothers run to local DHS offices putting our men on child support the first time the father does not do what they want or buy when they say buy. Some men need to be on child support and some prefer to be on child support, some men are good men and will take care of their children; however are burdened with child support. DNA testing is also a major issue. In this day and time it its really important to be absolutely sure that the alleged child (ren) is really the father's. My problem is how some parents go about finding out. "Grown folks" are going around bashing the other parent and denying the child (ren). IMMATURE. Why can't parents just go though the necessary steps and find out without all the extra excitement. With all do respect to "Maury"—why must we air our dirty laundry for the world to see and hear on national television? Who ever thinks about the children and how they will feel in the future when Maury has reruns. Children will embarrassingly see how crazy and foolish their parents acted. So many "grown folks" are busy trying to get their 15 minutes of fame; few take the children into consideration. The Black community admires and indulges in nonsense and drama as if it was a relevant fashion trend.

Negligent immature parents put their children off on who ever will take them without even inquiring the possibilities. Children are being sexually abused and parents are unaware because instead of monitoring their children they are worried about the absent parent. Some mothers are more in love with a man than their children and will over work themselves to wait on a man hand and foot, but put children on the back burner. Adolescents are roaming the streets aimlessly and parents do not know where these children are. Our community has too many broken homes. Parents are getting so wrapped up in their own lives they are misguiding and ignoring children. Adults have began to keep up with the latest in sports, news, gossip magazines etc but do not when reports come out or name at least 3 of their child's teachers. Parents are making it to the club and other social gatherings but cannot make it to parent teacher conferences. Guardians lust and fulfill their material wants with no interest in children needs. These misguided children grow into misguided and often angry adults. Child abuse is tied into negligence. "Child Help" recorded in the "National Child Abuse Statistics" that in the US there are over 3 million child abuse reports each year and can include multiple children. In 2007, approximately 5.8 million children were involved in an estimated 3.2 million child abuse reports and allegations. They also noted child abuse occurs at every socioeconomic level, across ethnic and cultural lines, within all religions and at all levels of education. Child physical and sexual abuse causes a long term effect on the abused children. Substance abuse, criminal behavior, and costly consequence keep the world on a downward whirlwind. VISIT: http://www.childhelp. org/pages/statistics and view the graphs, stats, and reports of child abuse and child neglect in America

Health Care

It is sad that any health risk of any kind is a killing our community. Not eating healthy and too busy focused on the wrong priorities is large percentage of the problem. People gripe and complain about the cost of a doctor visit-for those who go—and the cost of medicine but will spend hundreds of dollars on food and fashion monthly. Our women are more concerned about their hair than their health, our young men are to cool, and our men are too lazy or afraid. These are ridiculous reasons for our community health problems.

The eyes are often times bigger than stomach but people continue to consume all our eyes see. Gluttony has caused countless health problems. Over eating and too lazy to exercise or saying yes to seconds = a disappointing doctor visit. Americans participate and condone the ultimate gluttony: eating contest. Purposely over eating for prizes is disgusting, disgraceful, and abuse to ones body. People stuff their mouth with food while gagging and regurgitating and this country views it as entertainment but America is over eating and starving at the same time. Americans are so worried about the healthcare plan and what it will and will not cover yet are not helping to prevent preventable medical problems. Our community is leading in high blood pressure, diabetes, high cholesterol, heart attacks, and stroke due to irresponsible eating and irregular doctor visits.

Medical "break throughs" cause more harm than aid, killing us or leaving us worse off than we started; be that as it may, people think it is the cure for their irresponsible living. Why are the side effects worse than the original problem? Patients are destroying one part of the body while trying to repair another. Seeking a quick fix has some running to the doctor at every given chance. Doctors prescribe experimental medication and patients pop pills they have never heard of. If we would take better care of ourselves there would be no one running to law agencies because they took a drug that was recalled.

The Journal of the American Medical Association (JAMA) published an article emphasizing patient deaths with medical malpractice lawsuit statistics.

- 106,000 patients die each year from the negative effects of medication
- 80,000 patients die each year due to complications from infections incurred in hospitals
- 20,000 deaths per year occur from other hospital errors
- 12,000 people die every year as a result of unnecessary surgery
- 7,000 medical malpractice deaths per year are attributed to medication errors in hospitals
- These figure total 225,000 deaths each year, due to medical negligence of some nature. And that number is ever growing.

In 2006, a report was produced by the Institute of Medicine of the National Academies, stating that medication errors are one of the most common medical mistakes, causing injury or harm to at least 1.5 million people every year.

Health care providers can some time lead the ill wrong; nonetheless people need to take better care of THEMSELVES! People do not care about their bodies so why should a health care physician? Avoiding preventable health problems has to be taken more seriously in the Black community.

The Determining Factor

Where a person lives or comes from does not determine who they are or who they will become. So often our community blame behavior, way of living, and everything else wrong on upbringing and environment. "I live in da hood so that's why I have no vocabulary, no manners, no respect, and no self control and that is why I dropped out of school, sell drugs, fight, and shoot for no good reason." One's environment and family does play an active role in a person's outcome in life; however, at one point or another it becomes a choice. People so often blame other people for their actions and reactions, but a person CANNNOT make you do ANYTHING. No one can make anyone lie, commit crimes, drop out of school, fight, or have sex. Peer pressure has a hold on our community but the role models, the conformity, and the want to feel accepted is to blame. Statements like: "The only way to make it out the hood is to _____" has crippled our thinking and potential. Referring to neighborhoods as jungles and blaming the jungle because you act like an animal and all these beast, dogs, savages, gorillas, etc. make the world think or neighborhoods are a human zoo. Killing a person does not make anyone a beast; it makes him or her an idiot. Referring to oneself as an animal is often times used metaphorically but men are running around acting like characters from spider-man—goons and goblins, or are calling weaker individuals the most precious thing on a women's body. When did this become cool? Humans are at the top of the food chain, yet our community compares themselves to non-human creatures that can end up caged for display. We give America these descriptive words to describe the place so many of us call home and those adjectives and nouns are what America goes by.

The outcome of life can no longer be blamed on the surrounding of our community. Black neighborhoods across this country are rough and the everyday survival and struggle is intense, but who's to blame other than ourselves. The gorillas and goons cause the uproar, the violence, the crime and murder rate, the drop out rate, and negligence is the blame for teen pregnancy. Gangs around the country are ready to "go to war" over a simple disturbance. Bullets have no name, therefore innocent are harmed and affected by the anger, violence, and greed of Black communities nation wide.

MORE THAN FIT

CHAPTER 21

White supremacy has caused heavily drilled mental hurdles from the 16th century to present day times. The acts, behavior, attitudes, and structure of government have caused many Blacks to no longer strive for excellence. Negative thoughts and lazy behavior has our community in last-in more ways than one. By becoming bias against oneself, it allows the brain room for the racial lies. "WHAT YOU WERE IS WHAT YOU WILL ALWAYS BE" Although that is a LIE; too frequently Blacks give those people an advantage over us. Some assume because they are white they are automatically better, smarter, and faster, then cease trying when they are competition afraid those people will prevail over us. That adopted mentality is part of the reason the Black community is in the shape it is in. At the end of the day our people and those people are just that . . . people. Having good days & bad days, strengths & weaknesses, and ups & downs are the everyday for every living creature on this earth. The double standard between the races should be the only obstacle.

Our community has lost sight of the important. Ones personal "best" is all that is important regardless of where the Black community fails in society, at school, at work, in sports, academics, or social class. Comparing and judging oneself according to what whites are doing; keeps people compromising and living under an illusion. Comparing a persons' best to another is like comparing ones beauty and body to that of a model on a magazine cover. The Black community has to look at our community and ourselves and improve as BEST as we can.

AIN'T NOBODY BETTER THAN NOBODY

Europeans argued that they were superior to all others and the arrogant conquest and destruction of weaker races was only nature's way of improving the human species. This racial superiority was based on Darwin's ideas of survival of the fittest. With racial superiority becoming a conflict; nations and cultures competed with each other politically, economically, and militarily convinced that only the strongest would ultimately survive. White people will go to the ends of the earth to appear better and superior and willing to tell lie after lie until they and every body believe it. White people are not superior or better than any living species; they have no super powers; they are not the founders of North America; the slaves worked the land; they brought central government but the constitution and laws are manipulated everyday; they created a democracy that deceive the American people while convincing us we have power but don't. The true conclusion is those people are lying thieves.

Blacks are always looked down upon when it comes to Black history in America. Our history makes us who we are. I fully understand that Africans were brought to America by force to work the land and assist Europeans in building this country and after 400 years of that we began another struggle. The Black code, Jim Crow, separate but equal, integration, hate groups and crimes, the civil rights movement, and being Black in America left Blacks with more obstacles one can not imagine. Well that same history makes us some of the STRONGEST people in the world. We have survived all these years and from the looks of it we are only getting stronger. White people, especially the whites in history, knew this and that is why they have held on a bag of tricks to ensure struggle after struggle hoping that we would eventually fall. The song "We Shall Overcome" was sung because our people really believed in their hearts that our people where too great a people to remain at the foot of another man. We are still to great a people to accept any type of defeat by default.

IS BLACK REALLY BEATIFUL?

CHAPTER 22

It is no secret that once Adam ate the apple off the tree of life the world proceeded into destruction and although their eyes were open the world was blinded. [Adam is also responsible for fashion and cosmetics growth as a multi-billion dollar industry.]

To be naked be came shameful and to be beautiful and confident was to be clothed in expensive brands of clothing and jewelry. Fashion lines and Cosmetics Company feed off people(s) need to feel beautiful and accepted; that need sends people on an endless search for beauty that cannot be sold in stores. Blindness withholds the ability to see past a person's exterior. Humans natural beauty features, and abstract traits are unappreciated or unrecognized resulting in self-consciousness, self-absorption, and human contact is diluted with pretenses. This disobedience also gave way to stereotyping and bias thinking.

Our community is always trying to convince the world that Black is beautiful, but when you take an in depth look (at our women especially) beauty is not easily foreseen. In this century the stage has been set that any and all physical dislikes can be removed, enhanced, changed, or completely altered. As African Americans we stand a very unique people who come in different shades, shapes, and sizes. America does not see our diverseness as uniqueness and our community attempts uniformality. Perms, bleached colored hair, plastic surgery, skin lighteners, make-up, contact lenses, weave, eyelashes, nails etc are all products used in order to change appearance to suit society, peers, and the opposite sex.

Women have conformed to society's and/or hip-hop's definition of how a woman should look and what is considered to be "beauty." The appearance of Black ancestors conflicted with the modernization of the typical white women and sparked the transformation of the women throughout history. The closer a black woman was to white women the better she got treated. From physic to shade.

African American women decided to look nothing those women and began the transforming faze. Manageability and convenience are great but there are other prices paid. Heritage, culture, and identity are discarded without thought while silently saying the Creator made a mistake.

What are looks?

If one changes everything about who they are than whom does one become? Women during slavery were self-reliant leaders and women of many talents. Those women were looked upon by masters, family, elderly, men, children, and one another everyday with no room for miscellaneous distractions. Women of slavery were beautiful without fancy clothes and make-up. Complexion and hair had no bearing on those women and the burdens they bore compared to nothing of today's issues. Women of slavery were raped, beaten, mistreated, misused, bought, sold, and had to watch their families be treated in that manner and watch the men they loved and raised be treated as less than. Emotional support was all that could be offered due to ignorance and illiteracy. Although ignorant the women looked upon for food, clothing, healing, comfort, wisdom, and love from fellow slaves; Black women were doctors, nurses, scientists, chiefs, agriculturist, herbalist, psychiatrists, mothers, wives, musicians, inventors, garners, and servants unto the Lord and all those that needed them. They lived and died 400 years of hardship and survived. Those women had no time to worry about looks. They were beautiful in everyway by the heart and strength they displayed and are the most beautiful women of our culture. No product or surgery can give anyone that. Critics of then and now did not look beyond the surface nor did they judge past the exterior; nonetheless their physical features were who they were (Black women) and still who we are (Black women). Physical attractions are not automatically equivalent to beauty and who we naturally are (Black women) should not be masked nor compared to digitalized pictures.

BIG BOOTY JUDY

Sir-mix-alot's hit song "Baby Got Back" began the "big booty" phenomenon in 1992 and after 2 decades the fade of a big butt has boiled over into a way of life and women have gone to extreme measures to obtain the status of "big booty Judy."

Physical attributes of a woman have always been included in lyrics of hip-hop. Today's hip-hop artist associate physical with sexual while also generating the message that a certain weight, skin complexion, hair length, butt and breast size have to be met in order to be "wanted by men." Realistically the demand of a "big ass booty" can not be met by every woman due to physical and genetic make up; however that does not stop women from trying to meet the criteria.

The "big booty" fade has created a large space of insecurities in women about their over all appearance. Companies, plastic surgeons, crooks, and predators prey on any and all insecurities and with technology and medical advances the consumer market has been able to meet the demands of even the "ass." Booty pads, butt implants, butt injections, and butt supplements have granted women temporary and permanent fulfillment of a "big ass booty."

The visuals of entertainment have transformed relationships to only physical and sexual and the generations of men seek no abstract qualities in women. The use of women is more for display in hopes to influence their appearance of how they are viewed by peers and achieve and/or maintain the status of a "Bad Bitch" getter among peers. The need for attention drives women to become only physical attractions for the men they "represent." Women's desire to feel wanted added with misconceptions equals women who have allowed themselves to be tarnished mentally; women have allowed their self-esteem to be polluted and question self-worth from lack of "ass." "Ass and titties" are the focus while inter and outer beauty are ignored and tossed into the "careless" pile. A "fat ass" is not the only dimension a woman should credit herself with nor is it all that men should seek in a woman. The desire to feel wanted is not an abnormal emotion but the question is to what depth. A male(s) may want a woman for her "ass" but nothing beyond that point. Women are not catching the eye of possible husband material but rather mostly of males who have no long term intentions and who have no connection beyond physical and sexual. Men and women consumed by the culture of hip-hop are notorious for such a shallow way of thinking.

House or Field

How can Black be beautiful if a person is measured by their shade? Music once again widens the gap between women and promotes a bias message of what a Black woman should look like and how she should be treated. The existence of light vs. dark began long before hip-hop's birth and remains alive and well in the south. It is true that on many occasions lighter skinned Blacks—during slavery—got treated differently than darker skinned Blacks. The difference in treatment was various among situation due to envious attitudes, prejudices and egotistical thinking. During slavery-where the assortment of color began—a lighter shade Black American was obvious proof that Black and white had produced offspring and the teaching of white superiority resulted in more ignorance and discrimination among white and Black. To be born a mulatto-at that time—meant that one was still a slave however received consideration for the white genetics. A lighter work load, better treatment from whites, a different respect from Blacks, and a boost of self-esteem and ego brought a bridge between lighter skinned Blacks and darker skinned Blacks that has only become longer and wider over time.

To be in a dreadful position like slavery one would think their would be no acts of discrimination and prejudice among other slaves but it was. (It really made no sense to see one as more or less merely for having a white parent of grandparent. Most children had a slave mother and white father because the white men of that time had sex with slaves when they pleased no matter if either or both were married.) Mulatto offspring worked mostly in the house instead of the field as a claim to family ties. Not all house slaves were offspring from the master nonetheless field niggas were stereotyped as the darker slaves while house niggas were stereotyped as the lighter shade. House slaves—period—would sometimes get the mind set that they were better than the field slaves because they were cleaner and slightly better dressed than field hands. House slaves worked around the master's family daily and built relationships with the Big house and house slaves would be treated better morally than the field hands. To receive special treatment or earn the masters trust; house slaves would report the things going on among the slave community; like escape plans and other forbidden rules of the plantation. (Explains why it wasn't easy for slaves to take a stand.) Jealousy and favoritism intertwined with the endless curse of distress and oppression gave way to slave division and that problem has never completely been disassembled. The problem is rather petty yet causes problems in society, our community and our families. House or field, lighter or darker; they were still "nigger slaves" who were treated as less than to whites.

Society has made Blacks feel insecure about our color and we then go make matters worse; no matter what shade, we all have to check the box that reads "African American" which continues to put all of us in the same category in America's eyes. Mulatto=Black—the presidential election of 2008 made that clear.

God created man. Man reproduces man only because that is the way the Creator designed it. Offspring have control over themselves, their actions, and their destiny; however offspring have no control over their nationality, their place or time of birth, the parents who conceived them, the living conditions, standards or views imbedded in their mental foundation. Initial physical appearance was left to God until the point that man made alteration methods. Earthly sins have caused the earth to develop a widespread misunderstood judgmental outlook on one another because of clothed nakedness and has been sucked into material disparity. The origin of such tragedy began with disobedience, miscommunication, and deceit dating back to the book of Genesis. Deceit has grown to become the most powerful factor in the worlds despairing state.

The miscommunication lead to disobedience and opened a portal of evil with sin that continues to widen and has effected every generation from Genesis to the generations to come until Revelations is fulfilled.

MISTAKES

CHAPTER 23

Us vs. Ourselves

African-Americans live in an everyday struggle while battling "white" America. Blacks have errors in their ways—as does any and every human being in this world, but the repressed anger result in irrational and drastic behavior when released.

The Rodney King beating and riot which left a scar on the Black community, is one of those instances. In L.A. Black America was upset because despite visual proof of police brutality; the police were still found not guilty. Nationwide, Blacks where upset and outraged by America's justice system. Taking into consideration that the African-Americans in L.A. were pissed it still does not explain the point of the riot. Blacks and other participants destroyed, stole from and defaced their own neighborhoods, set a fire to local businesses, and hurt and stole from one another. The L.A. police beat Rodney K., they beat the trail, and then Blacks turn and beat each other. How much sense did that make?

Three days of violence rang out against people who had done no direct harm and the police were no where insight. People died, were injured, and even arrested. The nation sat in outrage over the beating, the trail, and misconduct of the LAPD; but the riot left the nation in surprise and in fear of Blacks. That riot was and still is the ammo that shots down the Black community. The best reaction to the situation is hard to answer but hurting each other was certainly not one of the best choices. Rioting did the government a favor by proving stereotypes to be true and also allowed them to make up new ones. Although that beating and riot was over 2 decades ago; our community beats and destroy one another on a daily basis. While we destroy and tear down one another, white America laughs and continues to treat us the way we treat one another. It has become an uphill battle against oppression in a dog eat dog—every man for himself world. Our community has become so angry and do not channel the anger at the source, but rather take it out on one another. We unleash all the pain, hurt, and confusion on any and every one; disregarding the common fact that all of us are angry on some level or another. People of our community have become lost wonderers with no feelings of belonging; The Black community is divided and left to fight the battle with society alone as individuals because we have rejected society, ourselves, and one another.

Is It Really Hate?

Forgiveness is sometimes hard especially when you feel you have been wronged repeatedly, however Black people are more forgiving than they realize and the Black community forgives the white community before we forgive ourselves.

How? We allow companies to rob us, cheat us out of our money, mistreat us on the job, stereotype us, lock us away for nonsense, discredit us, and give us poor service in social environments and we do nothing. We just take it. Ironically though, our community kills friends and neighbors over $40; not suggesting revenge on whites, but rather suggesting that we overlook one another's trespasses and transgressions at the same rate, if not more, as we do with those people. America thinks Blacks hate one another. Although that statement may be false in reality, the perception of that statement is true.

Perception is not reality nonetheless PERCEPTION EQUALS REALITY. At first glance it may seem like a misprint; next it may be hard to digest but no matter if America wants to face it or not, perception in America equals reality.

- Ex. Media of the mid 19th century was used to influence the thoughts of whites against Blacks in minstrel show and in early movie making.

Who Blacks were then and who they are now is still unrealistically portrayed in media; however, the influenced outlook of Blacks among all who receive and accept this deceitful information result in action through interaction. In reality Blacks may not be stupid lazy people but if the perception of Black people is that they are stupid and lazy; when Black interact with people who believe that, Blacks are treated like stupid lazy people and that perception has just became the reality of both parties.

- Ex. Whites used bias and racist scientific research, experiments, and studies to discredit Blacks value and their physical and mental capabilities in comparison to whites to get society to believe the lies.

This is also a physiological plot against Blacks and has had people to begin to perceive Blacks in accordance to scientific findings, then adopt and adapt to the conclusions of research and act on it. The perception may be a lie in comparison to the reality; however that will not stop the believers in displaying their perception of Blacks which then becomes the Blacks reality.

- Ex. Sports are often used to show that Black people have athletic abilities but still lack intelligence. Arguing that Blacks can play the game but are not fit to coach it.

That is yet another perception while the intelligence level and capabilities of Black potential coaches are never seen because of the perception. A fair measurement of true abilities would be the reality but one again the perception eliminates the possibility.—Hence why in the professional sports basketball and football players are predominately Black while majority coaches remain white.

Over time Blacks have undergone a hell of a history and the world wonders is their any love left in our community because the perception says that it is not. African-Americans stuck together during slavery but now broken homes and an unfair society has left our community on edge and a little crazy. Society perceives a community of hatred. I am not neglecting that our community commits acts of violence for various reasons that could sometimes come from hate but leaves the question *will there always be groups who hate Blacks and if so why is ok to hate Black people in America? As corny as this may sound: the only way to change our community is by displaying LOVE for ourselves and one another. We have to begin to really take care and genuinely look out for each other and our children. America has shown us she has no interest in us unless she is making profit and the past has shown us her ways of gaining profit are unlawful and damaging to those she uses. The perception that Black people hate one another is a lie and we can not believe what America and society says about us. That perception only leaves us to treat one anther the way America and society treats us. 1. What we see is what we believe 2. Then our thoughts become our words 3. Our words become our actions 4. Our actions become our destiny because PERCEPTION= REALITY.

Almighty

Love is oblivious in our community because God is no longer in our community. Our community has become worldly and filled with selfish desires that sometimes cause hate. We have lost our direction; leaving us lost in the world with out guidance or a leader. At one point our community was lead by Dr. King and other church leaders, practicing non-violence and working the Black community toward achievements but now our community is being lead by worldly people who do not know how to lead. Our figureheads are not worried about our community and its state, just themselves and money. A lot of Blacks attend church and are believers in Christ but it is hard to tell because of behavior and half of the people in the community who attend church are worse than the people who don't. Gossiping, lying, cheating, and stealing from one another is not the way God asked His people to live. Perfect is to far-fetched but efforts in self-control and personal behavior are ignored and misconduct is to often accepted by all—especially old. To many "adults" act like children misguiding their homes; People are too content and lazy to make a change or work toward a righteous life because it means that the things they enjoy doing—no matter how wrong—will have to be put away; People have become so selfish and careless about leading by example; and bad relationships, drug and alcohol abuse with God on the back burner has left generations of children distort, mislead, and unloved. The world takes no one into regard but itself and the world as a whole suffers especially the children in our community. People receive no love, affection, or attention at home and the world definitively is not going to provide it. People of the Black community wonder why; and the answer is often more clear and apparent but people would rather blame God.

Ex. Why as a kid did I have to watch my mom get beat?

People would love to blame God and walk around angry and choose to not believe and/or have little to no faith but it is not God's fault. Your mother had premarital sex and choose to be with who ever she ALLOWED to beat her. She decided to stay however long it happened and she is the one who that didn't provide you with the mental stability that you needed in order to not be so deeply scared.

No matter the question why; most times it was the people put in place to watch over us and protect us who hurt us. People do not want to hold their mom-or who ever—accountable for the bad experiences that they inflicted on them-especially if they have to accept personal responsibility. Parents get consumed in their selfish sinful lives and do not realizing the impact it has on children. We do not have control over every situation or any other person but we have complete and total control over ourselves. Instead of sweeping around our own front doors, we put blame on others and sweep around other peoples doors to make ourselves feel better. Christian married couples criticize worldly men and women for their lifestyle yet commit adultery against their spouse. Noting: all vowels are said before God. One generation after another it only gets worse and everyone wants to be known everywhere they go like life is a popularity contest but people have no relationship with the God of the most high. People know everything about everybody but do not know enough bout Jesus. How can we read gossip magazines, learn song lyrics, study for school, and work but do not learn about the One who knows everything about us. We worry about the judgment of others BUT on judgment day none of those people will be the Judge. Racism, prejudice, discrimination, lying, murder, rape, illegal activity, honesty, love, hate truth, integrity, and character all boil down to GOOD VS. EVIL. The world has been turned upside down; Evil is considered to be "acceptable," while righteous is critizied at every turn. How common evil has become should matter and help in realizing how twisted America has become. Christians are participating in scams and lies and going along with the world instead of what is right. Our community and country plaster and use God in everything yet act like He does not exist. "One nation under God," should be "One nation possessed by the Satan." There are churches scattered from corner to corner of this nation yet the world is filled with evil. Our community has been sucked into America's madness and she makes it look as if we are the cause of it all. God has to become who we are, Love has to become what we do, and righteous actions have to take place individually in every being in order to see a visual change across our community. The Black community has to care about its children and its neighbor instead of showing no regard for the fellow man. The presence, power, and love of God are all around but nobody takes the time out off their busy life to see it. Television, music, and the sins and evilness of people have swarmed our community with blindness and the truth about our Savior Jesus Christ. The world and the evil in it have driven the souls of man off the designed course and hell is waiting for those who do not accept certain truths.

THE REASON

CHAPTER 24

People are greedy and never satisfied and those people not only want feel superior; they want complete and total control over everything and everybody. Those people walk around as if special courtesies and exceptions should always be made on their behalf because of their color; Meanwhile they will ensure as much hardship and failure on others as possible. White people run this country and because of greed America is poisonous with a venomous government. They steal, kill, and destroy, and have been doing since the arrival to the continent. Evil is the root of racism, greed, the American government, discrimination, and bigotry. People have become knifing corruptors, which make them worse than the murders on the street. Murders can be caught and put away but corruptors can put innocent people away, keep guilty people on the streets, make trust worthy people steal, and make honest people liars. The realization of this country is, you do not have to be in politics or even be American to run this country, all you need is money. As long as you have money and get the white man in your pocket you gain power, influence, and control. Background, credibility, color, religion, or education matter none if the dollar amount is sufficient enough. MONEY = POWER&RESPECT.

The hue white symbolizes purity, cleanliness, good, and truth. Just because people are white does not mean they posses any of those traits. Colors have no feelings, no voice, and have no bearing on how we treat one another, every color was created on an equal scale, and every color is just as beautiful as the next and unique in its own way. Society has made an unbalanced scale of color and the general meaning by saying that every color is not unique and beautiful when it is the color of ones skin. Black and white are beautiful colors but becomes dark and hateful when referring to man.

Men of this world—all over this world—are heartless cold selfish beings who care only about material wealth even if it means starving everyone around them. Powerless beings of this world allow themselves to be deceived with thoughts of power and control by taking advantage of unaware, unprepared, uneducated, weak, trusting, and/or helpless victims through lies, manipulation, deceit, and violence. The world has become so cold and evil that man thinks that living and happiness is the American Dream and are willing to sell their souls to Satan in order to obtain that "Dream." That dream like many others in the world is an alluded reality that leaves predators in monstrous evil states of minds and prey deciding whether they should love or hate. Although the world has billions of people; there are only two sides-good and evil—and upon death there are only two place for the soul to rest—heaven or hell—and despite what people say or do every individual has to choose the life they decide to live and will have to give account for the life they lived on this twisted earth. LOOK BEYOND SELFISH DESIRES ask yourself the hard questions.